LEADERSHIP

700 Definitions and Ways to Lead

JOSEPH L. CURTIN

ARCHWAY
PUBLISHING

Archway Publishing books may be ordered through booksellers or by contacting:

Archway Publishing
1663 Liberty Drive
Bloomington, IN 47403
www.archwaypublishing.com
844-669-3957

ISBN: 978-1-6657-1897-4 (sc)
ISBN: 978-1-6657-1898-1 (e)

Library of Congress Control Number: 2022902895

Print information available on the last page.

Archway Publishing rev. date: 03/15/2022

To Joseph Rost and David Rosch, two of my leaders.

CONTENTS

ACKNOWLEDGMENTS

I am indebted to a number of people who contributed to the production of this book in one way or another throughout my life and since I began developing it in 2015. Thanks goes to all of the many librarians with whom I communicated all over the United States and in Great Britain, and to people who referred me to various sources of assistance both in person and in print. Especially helpful were Molly Dupere, Lindley Homol, and other members of the Northeastern University Library; Darren Townend and Dr. John Boneham of the British Library of the United Kingdom; and Abby Yochelson of the Library of Congress in Washington, DC.

In addition, I owe gratitude to the author of the book that is the standard to which I aspired, Joseph Rost; to a leadership professor at the University of Illinois who gave me helpful suggestions that began in 2016 and continued throughout publication, David Rosch; and to all of the other authors of leadership publications whom I believe have made the world a better place. I am thankful too for consulting clients, organizational managers and coworkers with whom I've worked who positively impacted my life; for athletic coaches who led me in elementary school, high school, and college; and for friends and relatives who have been supportive of me during the formulation and editing of this book as well as the years which preceded its publication.

INTRODUCTION

The first doctoral degree in leadership in the United States began in 1979 (University of San Diego, n.d.) with the help of Joseph Rost (International Leadership Association 2008), author of one of the most popular definitions of leadership. St. Catherine University (then the College of St. Catherine) began offering the first master's degree in leadership in 1986 (Clark, Freeman, and Gregory 1986), and the University of Richmond began offering the first undergraduate leadership major in 1992 (Freeman, Knott, and Schwartz 1994). By 2019, graduate programs and bachelor's degrees with majors and minors in leadership in higher education in the United States had grown in number to 1,178 (Guthrie, Batchelder, and Hu 2019).

In 2018, an estimated $3.5 billion was spent worldwide on leadership development, mostly by organizations (Training Industry 2019). In the words of Ron Riggio, Lifetime Achievement Award Honoree of the International Leadership Association (ILA) and author of the foreword of Bass and Bass (2008), stated at one of ILA's Annual Conferences, "Leadership goes where the money is and the organizations have the money that fuels the leadership industry" (R.

Riggio, personal communication, November 1, 2013). Despite the considerable financial and human resources expended on leadership development, no common definition of leadership exists (Rhodes and 't Hart 2014; Antonakis and Day 2018; Hughes, Ginnett, and Curphy, 2018; Yukl and Gardner 2020; Northouse 2022).

Rost (1991), author of one of the most popular definitions of leadership, lamented that too many different people and ways of doing things would be misidentified as leadership without a common definition. Bass and Bass (2008) proclaimed discovering and finding an accurate definition of leadership was hopeless. That appears to be the current state of affairs.

This book presents hundreds of people's definitions of leadership, a new definition of leadership, and a goal to attempt to achieve based on the definition. The problem with agreeing upon a common definition of leadership is that people are different. Nobody views the world and experiences life in exactly the same way. People are unique no matter how similar some of us are.

Readers of leadership publications are unique as well. Different readers have different expectations as to the benefit they wish to realize from the sources of information they read. Sometimes people read publications as means of acquiring a formal education. Sometimes people read to solve a specific problem. Other times people read to support or defend their own beliefs.

This book is based on the premise that it is important to define the what of something, its nature, before deciding how, the means, one will implement to attempt to achieve the what. Many of the 713 definitions quoted from 381 publications define leadership as action.

Whatever the goal of the reader, this book can provide a foundation upon which to base decisions to propose new ideas or to support or defend ideas communicated previously in an attempt to accomplish a new or established goal or to solve a new or recurring problem. Choices are freedom, and freedom is opportunity to achieve something better.

In 1974, Ralph Stogdill mused that a majority of those who defined leadership might have wished their definition would contribute something significant about leadership. My hope is that one or more of the definitions and the ways to lead cited in this book will help any student, teacher, author, consultant, executive, manager, supervisor, politician, voter, parent, teacher, friend, or lover to achieve a personal or professional goal.

CHAPTER 1

Review of the Literature

STOGDILL (1974), ALONG with quotes and paraphrases of leadership, leader, leadership acts, leadership behaviors, and how to lead, published quotes of thirty-eight definitions of *leadership* and *organizational leadership* he found from the time period 1906–1969. He grouped the definitions into eleven classifications that amounted to the leader as the center of all activity, the leader's character traits and how they affect others, accomplishing follower obedience, affecting others without coercion, one or more of a leader's actions, persuading others, possessing more power than another, leadership as a means of achieving goals, leadership as a product of the interaction between one with another or with a group, role being different from others, and providing organization for a group.

After Stogdill died, the second edition of *Handbook of Leadership* was completed by Bass (1981), who retained Stogdill's quotes, paraphrases, and classifications of *leadership, leader, lead*, and *power* definitions and descriptions, with a very slight modification of the name of one of the classifications and the addition of another category related to interactional effect.

In the third edition of *Handbook,* published in 1990, Bass maintained the number of leadership-definition quotes at thirty-eight, adding some more recent quotes of definitions of *leadership* and *leader* through 1987 while deleting some of the quotes from the two earlier editions. In addition, Bass added two more classifications related to leader power and freedom to act and a catchall category of multiple types of definitions, which he added to the two earlier lists of 1974 and 1981.

Rost (1991) quoted twelve leadership definitions from dictionaries he cited, which were published between 1828 and 1987, and he quoted 140 definitions of *leadership* from leadership scholars and practitioners that were published between 1927 and 1990. Only one definition of *leadership* appeared to be inaccurately cited—that of Webster (1828/1970)—although publications since Rost (1991) have cited the inaccurate reference. A definition of *leadership* was not published in Webster (1828) nor in Webster (1828/1970) which the Library of Congress confirmed in relation to the reprint of 1970 (A. Yochelson, personal communication, September 25, 2020). Worcester (1846) authored the first English-language definition of *leadership* published in a dictionary, after which Webster and Goodrich (1847/1848) published the second definition of *leadership* during the dictionary wars.

Also, Rost (1991) classified his definitions of *scholars* and *practitioners* into twenty-four categories of domination, control, authority, power; doing the leaders' wishes, trait; group; trait and group; Freudian; organizational; leader behavior; relationship; group facilitation; process; influence, effectiveness, and achievement of group and organizational goals; interaction; management; organizational behavior; attribution; exchange; political; functional; transformation; reality social construction; and empowerment.

Both Stogdill (1974) and Bass (1981) observed that various kinds of definitions were being published at the same time, but Rost (1991) created a timeline of types of definitions based on his analysis, which indicated to him a progression of definitions related to position authority, groups, behaviors, objectives, organizations, management, results, characteristics, perception, and delegation, to name a few.

Rost (1991) quoted two leadership definitions of United States Army's West Point Military Academy and reserve officers from the first three decades of the twentieth century. Possibly following the lead of Rost, a little over ten years later, Ciulla (2002) published her views about commonalities of leadership definitions per time period. In 2018, Ciulla expanded the definitions she had quoted or paraphrased sixteen years before, from two to a list of nine.

In addition to quoting the definition from Merch (M. B.) Stewart cited in Moore (1927) and the definition from Rost (1991), Ciulla (2018) added quotes of Bogardus (1934), Reuter (1941), Gibb (1954), Seeman (1960), Osborn and Hunt (1975), and Sarkesian (1981), as well as the ontology theory of Drath, McCauley, Van Velsor, O'Connor, and McGuire (2008) to represent her interpretation of leadership definition types by decades (1920–2010). Bass and Bass (2008) did not add more recently published definitional quotes and paraphrases of *leadership* from scholars and practitioners published in 1990 but did add more paraphrases of definitions of *leadership*, *leader*, and *lead*, including the paraphrasing of the international Globe Project's definition of *organizational leadership* (House, Javidan, Hanges, Dorfman, and Gupta 2004) while deleting others, renaming and separating some of the classifications of 1990, and adding the classifications of leader-centric definitions of *leaders* and *leadership*, attribution, symbol, making of meaning, thought, effect of interaction, process, and identification with the leader, consolidating all twenty-one into leader's characteristics, leader's actions, leader's results, and the leader-follower interaction.

Also, breaking from Stogdill (1974) and emulating the leadership-by-decade time period of Rost (1991), Bass and Bass (2008) characterized definitions of *leadership* by decades beginning with 1920–1929 and ending with 2000–2009 as leader domination power, process effect, group effect, influence effect, power or freedom to act, inspiration, change intention, and executive position, respectively.

Stogdill (1974), Bass (1981, 1990), and Bass and Bass (2008) did not reference all the publications they reviewed in order to publish their presentation of leadership definitions and classifications. Consistent with the process of transforming inputs into outputs generally recognized as operations management by management scholars (Daft 2018; Robbins and Coulter 2018), Rost (1991) reported inputs of 221 leadership definitions he studied and discovered in nearly six hundred publications.

CHAPTER 2

Method

ALL THE ESTIMATED 1,750 English-language or English-translated books, book chapters, journal articles, and websites reviewed from 2015 to 2021 for this study, which were thought capable of presenting a definition of *leadership, organizational leadership*, or *political leadership*, are not included within the references list of this book. However, an exception was made in the case of some dictionaries that were researched and included in the bibliography.

Quotes of definitions and contexts by author, publisher, or person quoted or interviewed; the dates of original publication, such as Adolf Hitler, whose original work of volume 1 was published in 1925 in German and translated into English (Murphy 1939); the interpretations of the definitional and contextual quotes; and the categorizations of the definitional quotes based on the interpretations were acquired. Identical definitions published by the same first author in multiple works were eliminated from categorization due to redundancy. An effort was made to include words of definitions that indicate what leadership is.

Some authors defined *leadership* in multiple ways. For example, in his book within the context of political leadership, Burns (1978/1979) stated three definitions of *leadership* on pages 18, 19, and 425. Because all three definitions were included within the same publication, three definitions were analyzed, and all three definitions were categorized within one or more of the categories of classification.

To the extent believed possible, specific theories, models, and approaches or any other subsets of leadership were eliminated from classification, because these were determined to be specific ways in how to lead or how one should lead or did lead, as opposed to what leadership is and the nature of leadership. For example, Reuter (1941) provided a specific type of definition related to creativity in addition to his general definition of *leadership*. Both definitions were analyzed. However, only the general definition of *leadership* was categorized. Definitions of *general*, *organizational*, or *political leadership* included within publications that proposed or supported a specific theory, model, or approach were classified. For example, Burns (1978/1979) presented multiple subsets of his political leadership definitions, which were analyzed, but none of those definitions were classified.

An attempt was made to include definitions of leadership which met selection criteria from organizations such as the United States Department of the Army and people who had held or were serving in management positions in private enterprise and public institutions who were interviewed and quoted such as John Burns, Governor of the United States State of Hawaii, David Davenport, President of Pepperdine University, Dwight Eisenhower, President of the United

States, Adolph Hitler, German Chancellor and Fuhrer, Marshall Loeb, Managing Editor of *Fortune* Magazine, Ross Perot, 1992 United States Presidential Candidate and Founder and Chairman of The Perot Group, Robert Reich, United States Secretary of Labor, William Solomon, Chairman and CEO of Austin Industries, and Merch (M. B.) Stewart, General in the United States Department of the Army in addition to authors and university professors such as Peter Senge of the MIT Sloan School of Management and Ordway Tead of the Columbia University Graduate School of Business.

Definitions stated in primary sources of publication were included in the study. Most of the quotes are from dictionary authors and publishers and nondictionary authors, such as scholars and practitioners, with the exception of a few quotes of scholars and organizational practitioners quoted by trusted authors. To the extent believed possible, only words of publications that presented definitions of *leadership* in general and of certain subtypes of leadership, such as *organizational leadership* and *political leadership*, are cited.

Rost (1991) commented on the reluctance of authors writing about leadership within the environments of politics, education, and business to define *leadership* in general. However, the aim of this study was to provide the foundation on which to base a universal definition of *leadership* applicable within all contexts, political leadership of the electorate and political organizational leadership of governmental employees, educational organizational leadership, business organizational leadership, and informal leadership within all contexts. An overarching definition of *leadership* was sought. People follow specific organizations and political, religious, spiritual, and other types of doctrines in addition to individuals, although it is true some people will leave organizations to follow a specific individual to another organization and abandon a doctrine in an attempt to improve their situation.

Dictionaries researched and reviewed for this study were selected from the English and American dictionaries referenced in Steger (1913), Starnes and Noyes (1946), Landau (2001, 2009), Cowie (2009), and Bejoint (2010), beginning with the first dictionary of the English language, the British dictionary authored by Cawdrey, which was published in 1604.

Three reasons accounted for the review of dictionaries and inclusion of some dictionary definitions in the categorization. First, scholarly definitions of *leadership* published in nondictionary sources before 1900 were not found. However, leadership was defined by some dictionaries prior to 1900. Second, before definitions of *leadership* were published in English and American books and scholarly journals, the earliest dictionary authors were the lay scholars of their day. Noah Webster, the most famous American dictionary author, was a schoolteacher, as was the earliest popular-dictionary definer of *leadership*, Joseph Worcester (Starnes and Noyes 1946; Landau 2001; Bejoint 2010). Chauncey Goodrich, who began editing Webster's dictionaries beginning with Webster (1841), was a professor of rhetoric (*Archives at Yale*. nd. https://archives.yale.edu/repositories/12/resources/3046) and oratory at Yale University (Steger 1913). Educators dominated the field of lexicography from the beginning of English monolingual dictionary making (Landau 2001) until the mid-nineteenth century (Starnes and Noyes 1946). Finally, in selecting authors and editors who headed dictionaries that were among the first to define *leadership* and related terms, the analysis of definitions could attempt to determine changes in definitions over time since the very first definitions in the 1800s. Publishers of monolingual English dictionaries responded to and continue to respond to changes in the market preferences of the consumers who purchased the dictionaries. The goal was to select dictionaries that were believed to indicate an evolution of the word *leadership* as influenced by dictionary authors/editors and publishers over time.

Dictionary definitions of leadership included within the final categorization of definitions were two authored and edited by Worcester (1846, 1860); six definitions published by the company of George and Charles Merriam beginning in 1847/1848, now named Merriam-Webster; two published by the Century Company, the first in 1889/1991 and the second in 1927, which formed the basis of the early dictionaries published by both World Publishing and Random House; three published by Random House beginning in 1947; two from World Publishing, publisher of a line of *Webster's New World* dictionaries that competed effectively against Random House beginning in 1951 (especially in the college-dictionary market beginning in 1953) and continues to be published to this day by Houghton Mifflin Harcourt; four dictionaries beginning in 1969 of the American Heritage line, which was acquired by Houghton Mifflin/Houghton Mifflin Harcourt; three beginning in 1908 by Clarendon Press, the publisher of *The Oxford English Dictionary*; and three Funk and Wagnalls dictionaries beginning in 1893 (Landeau 2001, 2009).

Only one dictionary, *Encarta Webster's Dictionary* by Bloomsbury, one of the first of the intermediate-sized dictionaries to accomplish successful market results in the American market (Landeau 2001, 2009), was included in the study and was not among the dictionary lines of dictionary author Worcester and the publishers Merriam

Brothers/Merriam-Webster, Century Company, Clarendon Press, Funk and Wagnalls Company, Random House/Penguin Random House, World Publishing/Houghton Mifflin Harcourt, and American Heritage/Hougton Mifflin Harcourt.

Dictionary definitions of popular English and American English dictionaries selected for analysis were believed to represent a credible sample of *leadership* definitions indicating a reflection of what leadership was in the days the dictionaries were published. If subsequent editions of market-effective brands of popular dictionaries contained duplicate definitions of earlier definitions, the duplicate definitions were not included in the 366 definitions selected for categorization and determination. Identical definitions of some dictionaries published by two or more different publishing companies were included. However, leadership definitions of different editions of the same dictionary line and those of same publisher were excluded. For example, Porter (1890), the editor of a dictionary published by G. and C. Merriam Co. within which *leadership* was defined, presented the exact same words as Worcester (1846), which published the very first definition of *leadership* over forty years previously. Because Porter (1890) and Worcester (1846) were published by different dictionary lines, both of those identical definitions were classified. However, the definition of *leadership* in the first edition of *Webster's Collegiate Dictionary* (1898), published as an abridgement of Porter (1890) for college students by the same company, G. and C. Merriam Co., was not classified because it was an exact duplication within the same dictionary line.

Nondictionary publications researched and reviewed for this study were selected at random for the most part, with the exception of some of the publications referenced in Stogdill (1974), Bass (1981,

1990), and Bass and Bass (2008), which are the first four editions of *The Handbook of Leadership*, and in Rost (1991). Some of the authors referenced in those five books were excluded from categorization for failure to meet inclusion criteria. For example, definitions of leaders were not classified in this study—only definitions that were interpreted as describing what leadership is.

Words within published nondictionary definitions were interpreted and categorized by commonality of nature. Some nondictionary publications offered definitions of terms used within the definitions. Greenleaf (1972) and Tannenbaum, Weschler, and Massarik (1961) are two of the publications that defined terms used within their respective definitions of *leadership*.

Some publications did not appear to define terms, however. For example, *leadership* was defined in some publications as the noun *dynamic*. However, the word *dynamic* was not defined explicitly within the publication that defined *leadership* as a dynamic.

In other cases, authors used terms within definitions which appeared to conflict with common understandings of the words. A conscious effort was made to interpret words as authors intended, though. For example, the word *personality* was used within one of the definitions of *leadership* (See Gibb 1947 in the Appendix, in Table 1) but within the same publication Gibb (1947) stated "leadership is not an attribute of the personality but a quality of his role" (267).

Inclusion and meanings of words change because words defined in dictionaries are based on citations gathered over time (Landau 2001). Because words have been in use for a period of time before dictionary publication, words of nondictionary author's definitions of the nature of leadership were interpreted and classified in accordance with definitions from a number of dictionaries in an effort to interpret and classify words appropriately according to the times within which the nondictionary authors lived.

Popular dictionaries as determined by Landau (2001, 2009), Cowie (2009), and Bejoint (2010) were selected for interpreting and classifying all of the definitions selected for this book. The dictionaries used for interpreting words of leadership definitions and the contexts for those definitions that were acquired for this study included the popular dictionaries of Vizetelly (1922); Funk and Wagnalls, the fiercest competitor of G. and C. Merriam from 1890 to 1930 (Landau 2001; Cowie 2009; Landau 2009); Friend and Guralnik (1953), based on the successful competitor of G. and C. Merriam/ Merriam-Webster, published by the World Publishing Company in 1951; Friend and Guralnik's *Webster's New World Dictionary of the American Language Encyclopedic Edition* (Landau 2009); Gove (1961), the last of the great unabridged dictionaries in America (Landau, 2009), offering approximately 450,000 words (Bejoint 2010) on 2,262 third-edition pages; Barnhart (1963), a 2,265-page, two-volume dictionary of approximately 200,000 words (Bejoint, 2010); and Gove (1963), the seventh edition of *Merriam-Webster's Collegiate Dictionary* series, based on Gove (1961).

Other popular dictionaries used for interpretation and classification of leadership definitions included Costello (1991) based on the successful 1987 second edition of *Random House Dictionary*, which was the beginning of effective marketplace responses to dictionaries published by G. and C. Merriam/Merriam-Webster (Landau, 2009); *Collegiate Dictionary* series by G. and C. Merriam/ Merriam-Webster, published in the wake of Gove (1961), Mish (1993/1994), and Mish (2003/2014), of which the tenth and eleventh editions originated with the dictionary of G. and C. Merriam in 1898;

and Kleinedler (2014/2018, 2016), which are fifth editions of Friend and Guralnik's dictionaries of 1951 and 1953, respectively; and Pickett (2011/2018), the fifth edition of a series of dictionaries begun in 1969 in market-competition response to Gove (1961) (Landau 2009).

Most of the publications of definitions of *leadership* contained words that indicated a large number of the authors analyzed believed leadership is a behavior, a process, an interaction, a characteristic or characteristics, an ability, a concept, an effect, a phenomenon, a role, a function, a state, or a relationship. Vizetelly (1922) defined *behavior* more along the lines of conduct but did include the word *action* as a synonym of the word *behavior*. Friend and Guralnik (1953) defined *behavior* as a verb by adding the suffix -*ing*, included *behavior* as an action, and echoed that of Vizetelly (1922) in relation to the word *conduct*. The definition of *behavior* in Gove (1961) mirrored the definitions of *behavior* of Vizetelly (1922) and Friend and Guralnik (1953) but was much more comprehensive and wide-ranging because he incorporated psychological and instinctual labels to what was taking place in relation to those involved, and he was more social in definition by adding the concept of reaction within a context of social interaction in addition to individuals taking action and performing anything at any given point in time.

Gove (1963) included words that indicated leading, directing, guiding, and escorting another, and he defined *leading* as part of his definition of *behavior*. Barnhart (1963) stuck to the basics of action. All four dictionaries appeared to indicate that behavior is action.

Dictionaries published later that were referenced for this study did not deviate from *behavior* defined as action (Costello 1991/1992; Mish 1993/1994; Mish 2003/2014; Pickett, 2011/2018; Kleinedler 2014/2018, 2016).

Process was defined by Vizetelly (1922) in part using verbs and nouns that indicated *produce, course, method, series, production,* and *happening.* In addition to some of the words Vizetelly (1922) used to define process, Friend and Guralnik (1953) added words that amounted to *doing* and *continuing.* Gove (1961) defined *process* extensively and very specifically, defining *process* using words that were similar to or identical to words used by the aforementioned dictionaries, but adding words that indicated *process* is an action, forward movement, progress, completing something, successive acts, events, stages, experience, advancement, phenomena, conditions, changes over time, transformation, a system, or an accomplishment. Gove indicated the word was used most frequently in description of the way things were achieved in manufacturing a product. For his collegiate dictionary, Gove (1963) shortened much of his earlier definition of *process* published in Gove (1961). In addition to using some of the same words as other dictionaries in the past, Barnhart (1963) indicated *process* is also more than one action, and change and was unique in progression.

Over the years, the definition of *process* doesn't seem to have evolved significantly in the dictionaries from Vizetelly (1922), Friend and Guralnik (1953), Gove (1961), and Gove (1963). After the definitions published in earlier dictionaries, only a few words were added in definition of *process,* such as words that indicated *process* is one or more steps or functions in movement toward an end result, with a couple of dictionaries echoing the use of the word in relation to the manufacturing of some product (Costello 1991/1992; Mish 1993/1994; Mish 2003/2014; Pickett, 2011/2018; Kleinedler 2014/2018, 2016).

Interaction was not defined in Vizetelly (1922), but Friend and

Guralnik (1953) defined *interaction* using words that indicated *interaction* is one acting on another and affecting each other in reciprocity. Gove (1961) added words that indicated mutuality and the two or more changing each other. Barnhart (1963), Costello (1991/1992), Mish (1993/1994), and Mish (2003/2014) added nothing new to earlier definitions. Kleinedler (2016) did not define *interaction*, but Kleinedler (2014/2018) added the concept of cooperation to the meaning of *interaction*. Pickett (2011/2018) added nothing new.

Action was defined in part by Vizetelly (1922), who used words that indicated something being done, work, operating, someone or something being active in some way, and behaving or conducting themselves voluntarily or rationally. The concept of something being done voluntarily or rationally in way of definition of the word *action* in an American publication of 1922 may have indicated consistency with American culture at that time. Friend and Guralnik (1953) added noting in addition to Vizetelly (1922), but Gove (1961), within a context applicable to *leadership*, added words that indicated *action* is forcefully altering or changing something or someone, either mentally or physically, in an organized manner energetically, and he included words indicating one that is performing, initiating, and conducting oneself in some way. Gove (1963) added the concept of difficulty of undertaking for whatever reason to the definition of Gove (1961). Barnhart (1963) defined *action* using words that were consistent with earlier definitions of *action*, *interaction*, and *process*.

Costello (1991/1992), in definition of *action*, added descriptors that indicated consciousness, practicality, habitualness, and normalcy. Mish (1993/1994) added the potential of repeating something to possible definitions of *action*. Mish (2003/2014) and Kleinedler (2016) added nothing new, but Kleinedler (2014/2018) added movement to potential definitions of *action*, as well as the characteristic of being bold. Pickett (2011/2018) stressed goal accomplishment, exertion, and vigor and even indicated *action* could be defined as using power to cause modification of something or someone.

Although an attempt was made to achieve consistency and standardization in relation to interpretation of the words published for classification, some words were interpreted differently. Most authors did not define all of the words of the terms within definitions. For example, the term *function* appeared to possess different meanings for different authors. To the extent possible, the word *function* was interpreted three different ways based on the context within which the word was used. Some authors like Tannenbaum, Weschler, and Massarik (1961) did define their terms and did define the word *function*, and in the case of their definition of *leadership*, the word *function* was interpreted to mean action.

Another way the word *function* was interpreted in this publication and the definition of *leadership* classified in total or in part was as a role or an effect of actions and situation. The word *function* appeared to be used in most of the leadership definitions to indicate leadership as a role. In other instances, though, it appeared authors of leadership definitions intended the word *function* to signify leadership as an effect, as seemed to be the case in Avolio (2007). (See Avolio 2007 in the Appendix, in Table 1). Within the context of Avolio (2007), the word *function* was interpreted as an effect rather than a role.

Another word that was interpreted in multiple ways was *influence*. Although most authors seemed to indicate the word *influence*, as used within a definition of *leadership*, was intended to mean the effect of one on another or others, there were exceptions. Osborn and Hunt (1975), for example, defined *leadership* using the word *influence*, which was classified as action because doing so was believed to be consistent with the way the authors would have wanted the word *influence* to be interpreted.

Words of publications interpreted as defining *leadership* or elements of leadership as behavior, process, or interaction within the context in which those words were used were categorized within the classification of action. Words that appeared to indicate leadership is action are listed in the appendix, in Table 2.

The same process that was detailed in paragraphs previously to describe how the classification of action was determined using popular dictionaries spanning nearly one hundred years was used to decide upon the other six classifications of characteristic, concept, effect, phenomenon, role, and state. Many publications in which *leadership* was defined contained words that indicated a large number of the authors analyzed believed leadership is either characteristics, an ability, or both. Publications that were interpreted to define *leadership* or elements of leadership as a characteristic or ability were categorized within the classification of characteristic. Words that were interpreted as defining *leadership* as one or more characteristics within the context of the publication are listed in the appendix, in Table 2.

Some publications that defined *leadership* contained words that indicated a significant percentage of nondictionary authors analyzed believed leadership is a concept. Words that were interpreted as defining *leadership* as a concept within the context of the publication are listed in the appendix, in Table 2.

Some publications that defined *leadership* contained words that indicated a significant percentage of the authors analyzed believed leadership is an effect. Words that were interpreted as defining *leadership* as effect within the context of the publication are listed in the appendix, in Table 2.

Some publications that defined *leadership* contained words that indicated a number of the authors analyzed believed leadership is a phenomenon. Words that were interpreted as defining *leadership* as a phenomenon within the context of the publication are listed in the appendix, in Table 2.

Some publications that defined *leadership* contained words that indicated a number of the authors analyzed believed leadership is a role or function. Words that were interpreted as defining *leadership* as a role within the context of the publication are listed in the appendix, in Table 2.

A significant percentage of publications that defined *leadership* contained words that indicated a number of the authors/publishers included within this study believed leadership is a relationship or, to a lesser degree, a state. Words that were interpreted as defining *leadership* as a state within the context of the publication are listed in the appendix, in Table 2.

After an interpretation of all of the words in definitions of *leadership* selected for inclusion within the study, the scheme of classification was as follows: action, characteristic, concept, effect, phenomenon, role, and state. Interpretation of words was difficult at times. For example, the word *dynamic* as a noun in the singular form, which was used rarely in a *leadership* definition, was not present in dictionaries published earlier such as Vizetelly (1922) and Friend and Guralnik (1953), but it was present later in others such as Gove (1961), Barnhart (1963), and Gove (1963). However, popular dictionaries published in more recent times like Mish (1993/1994) and Pickett

(2011/2018) defined *dynamic* somewhat differently from the earlier popular dictionaries published from 1922 to 1963.

Many publications appeared to present words that defined *leadership* in multiple ways, which resulted in that publication being classified in more than category. For example, Bogardus (1934), the first to publish the word *followership* in the leadership literature, stated words in multiple definitions of *leadership*, which indicated leadership is action, one or more characteristics, an effect, or a phenomenon. Therefore, the definitions of Bogardus (1934) met the criteria for inclusion within more than one category.

Performance was another word that was interpreted in multiple ways. For example, sometimes performance was interpreted as an effect because some of the definitions of leadership amounted to the performance of individuals or groups as a result of influence, as was the apparent case of some of the definitions of Drucker (1954) and Dansereau, Yammarino, Markham, Alutto, Newman, Dumas, Naughton, Kim, Al-Kelabi, Lee, and Keller (1995). In other publications, the word *performance* was interpreted merely as action regardless of someone's believed influence, as was the apparent case of the definition of Fiedler (1965), which included one's direction and supervision, and that of one of the definitions of Mumford (2011).

The word *leading* possesses the suffix *-ing*, a present participle and a form of a verb expressing the present action of another word (Pickett, 2011/2018; Prcic, 2008). The base word of *leadership* is *leader*, which possesses the suffix *-er*, the noun form of the verb *lead*. Strict rules of grammar were not applied in all cases because some words within the context of use were interpreted differently. Table 2 in the appendix lists the words that were interpreted and the manner in which those words were classified.

CHAPTER 3

First English-Language Dictionary Definitions of Leadership and Other Words Related to Leadership

THE EARLIEST AUTHORITATIVE definitions of *leadership* were published in some dictionaries before those published in scholarly journals and credible books after 1900. Some of the definitions of *leadership* in the earliest English and American dictionaries researched and analyzed contained the words *follow, follower, following,* and *followership,* in addition to the words *lead, leader, leading,* and *leadership.*

As would be expected from words published many years ago, some of the words spelled in both English and American dictionaries were not spelled the same as those words exist now in the English language. For example, what was interpreted as the word *modification* was spelled differently in the definition of the word *state* in Webster and Goodrich (1847/1848) than the word is spelled currently in dictionaries today.

The earliest dictionaries of the English language were British. Cawdrey (1604) did not state definitions for any of the eight English leadership-related words of *lead, leader, leading, leadership, follow, follower, following,* and *followership* (D. Townend, personal communication, September 28, 2020); neither did Bullokar in 1616 (J. Boneham, personal communication, December 12, 2020), Cockeram (1623/1930), Blount (1656/1972), Phillips (1658), and Coles (1676/1971). However, the anonymous author of *Gazophylacium Anglicanum* (1689/1969) was the first to publish a definition of one of the words: "follow … to follow after" (p. "FO"). The word *lead* was first defined as "to lead one by the Hand" (Kersey 1713, "LE") and *follower* was first defined as "One who follows or waits upon" (Bailey 1727, "FO"). Later, Martin (1749, "LEA") defined the word *leader* first with "a guide, or conductor … a chief, or general … the person that plays first at cards."

Leading was first defined in a dictionary as "principal" and "Principal" by Scott and Bailey (1755, "LEA") and Johnson (1755, "LEA"), respectively. Webster (1841), the development of which was supervised by Noah Webster's son-in-law, Chauncey Goodrich, and edited by Joseph Worcester because the publisher, S. Converse, and Goodrich wanted a smaller dictionary and because Webster was not feeling well during the last thirteen years of his life before dying two years later in 1843 (Micklethwait 2000), was the first to define the word *following*, as "Coming or going after or behind; pursuing; attending; imitating; succeeding in time; resulting from as an effect or an inference; adhering to; obeying, observing; using, practicing; proceeding the same course … Being next after; succeeding" (698).

Many dictionaries did not and still do not cite early dates of use of the word *leadership*, upon which definitions of *leadership* are based. However, Random House, Merriam-Webster, and Clarendon Press published dictionaries that cited information related to early use of the word *leadership* in the English language. Although the word was not defined, Oxford University Press claimed the word *leadership* was first used in a letter written by C. W. Wynn in 1821, and the second use of the word *leadership* was within a newspaper article written by Albany Fonblanque, a political journalist and journal editor, in 1834 (Oxford University Press, 2000-. https://www-oed-com.ezproxy.neu. edu/view/Entry/106604?redirectedFrom=leadership#eid).

Mish (2003/2014), the most recent dictionary of Merriam-Webster when this publication went to press, has a date of first use of the word *leadership* as 1821 also, but no information from the publisher was forthcoming despite numerous phone and email requests. Costello (1991/1992) published a date of 1815–1825 in relation to the first documented use of *leadership*, but Penguin Random House, the current publisher of the dictionary, was unable to locate information related to the dates (B. Dreyer, personal communication, May 10, 2021).

Noah Webster's first dictionary was published in 1806, and the second, *An American Dictionary of the English Language*, was published in 1828. Many dictionary scholars have acclaimed the second edition as the first great American dictionary written by the most important lexicographer in the history of the United States (Steger 1913; Green 1996; Landau 2001, 2009; Cowie 2009; Bejoint 2010). According to Green (1996), Noah Webster was the first to use the term *American language* but neither of Webster's first two dictionaries published a definition of *leadership*.

Neither did Webster's third dictionary, copyrighted in 1840 by both Joseph Worcester and Webster and published in 1841. Fierce competition and economics influenced the earliest definitions of *leadership* published in dictionaries. S. Converse, the publisher of

Webster's 1828 classic dictionary, which Webster wanted priced at twenty dollars to reflect the quality of the publication, wanted a less expensive abridgment to compete against smaller dictionaries in the marketplace (Micklethwait 2000). In 1828, $20 was the equivalent of over $550 in 2021 according to the US Bureau of Labor Statistics (E. Karageorge, personal communication, April 19, 2021).

In 1829, with Webster's approval, Converse persuaded Joseph Worcester, who was working on his own dictionary at the time, to edit the first revision of Webster (1828). Chauncey Goodrich, Webster's son-in-law, was interested in profitability too and agreed a smaller dictionary was best. After Webster's health began to fail, Goodrich took over management of Webster's dictionaries published in 1841 and 1847/1848 (Micklethwait 2000). Thus, the stage was set for the dictionary wars of 1834–1864, which began when Webster attacked Worcester for plagiarism in 1834, continued after Webster's death in 1843, and ended a year before Worcester's death in 1865 (Landau 2001, 2009). During that time, the first two popular-dictionary definitions of *leadership* were published by Worcester (1846) and Webster and Goodrich (1847/1848).

Consistent with the first documented use of the word *leadership*, used to characterize it as a formal position of political power, Worcester (1846) published the first popular-dictionary definition of *leadership* (see the appendix, in Table 1); defined *leader* as "He or that which leads; a chief; a commander; the principal wheel in machinery; the foremost horse in a team" (413); and defined *office* as "the station, condition, or employment of an officer; a public charge or employment; magistracy; agency; business; function; peculiar use; charge; duty; service; benefit; act of worship; formulary of devotions: a room, house, or place of business" (494). The inclusion of the word *horse* in dictionary definitions of *leader* continues to this day (Pickett 2011/2018; Merriam-Webster, n.d.).

In Webster and Goodrich (1847/1848), published by G. and C. Merriam Co. at the lower price of six dollars (Merriam-Webster, n.d., https://www.merriam-webster.com/about-us/faq), Goodrich was the second dictionary author and editor to define *leadership* (see the appendix, in Table 1); defined the word *state* as "condition; the circumstances of a being or thing at any given time. These circumstances may be internal, constitutional, or peculiar to the being, or they may have relation to other beings" (1079); and defined the word *condition* as "state; a particular mode of being ... quality; property; attribute ... state of the mind; temper; temperament; complexion" (244).

Worcester (1860) included the word *state* in his second definition of *leadership*, published in the second edition of his dictionary (see the appendix, in Table 1), and defined *state* as "condition as determined by whatever circumstances; the circumstances under which any being or thing exists; situation; position; predicament; case; plight ... Stationery point; point from which the next movement is regression; crisis; height ... estate; seignoiry; possession" (1047). Another dictionary author, Whitney (1889–1891, 3385), was the first to add the components of *guidance* and *control* to the lexicon of *leadership* within his definition, and Funk (1893, 1011) was the first to contribute the characteristic "ability to lead" to a definition of *leadership*.

Although the word *followership* was defined for the first time within the leadership literature by Bogardus (1934), the first popular major American English dictionary to publish a definition of the word *followership* was Gove (1961, 883), who defined the word as "the body of followers of a leader: FOLLOWING ... the capability of following a leader or obeying authority."

CHAPTER 4

Results

THE AIM OF this study was to produce a definition of *leadership* agreeable to the general public, scholars, practitioners, and others by accepting and interpreting the what of *leadership* within definitions of *leadership* stated in publications of scholars, organizational managers in business, government and nonprofits, politicians, consultants, popular-dictionary authors, editors, publishers, and others, and by classifying the publications' definitions within categories of interpretation of what the publications stated leadership is (see the appendix, Table 1).

Three-hundred eighty-one popular-dictionary and nondictionary publications containing definitions met inclusion criteria and were classified. Twenty-seven of the 381 publications were popular dictionaries published as early as 1846 and as late as 2004. The dictionary definitions were categorized after a review of hundreds of dictionaries. Dictionaries cited in Table 1 are denoted by an asterisk after the name or names of the author or editor assumed to possess the most authority and responsibility for the publication.

The definitions as interpreted were found to define *leadership* in total or in part as an action or actions, a characteristic or characteristics, a concept, an effect, a phenomenon, a role and a state, although no dictionary or nondictionary publication stated definitions that were determined to be included within one or more of the seven categories of classification. Twenty-four of the twenty-seven dictionaries (nearly 90 percent) published definitions of *leadership* that were interpreted and categorized within multiple classifications. The same held true for 354 nondictionary authors, although the percentage of publications interpreted as presenting definitions that were interpreted to be included within multiple classifications was much lower, at 52.3 percent. Nearly 48 percent of the publications were interpreted as presenting definitions that were determined to be included within one classification only. Stogdill (1974) stated nearly fifty years previous that some of the definitions he listed in his reference could have been categorized in multiple classifications, of which he had eleven.

The words published by authors, editors, and publishers that were interpreted appear in the appendix, in Table 2. As stated earlier, sometimes the same word used within a definition of *leadership* was interpreted differently due to the context, the manner in which the word was written.

The classifications of *leadership* definitions as published in popular dictionaries from 1922 to 2004; in nondictionary books, book chapters, articles; and on websites appear in the appendix in Table 3. By a wide margin, leadership definitions classified as action were presented most often in the 381 publications—nearly 70 percent. Leadership as one or more characteristics were second in number, reaching a percentage total of 31.8, followed by leadership-as-effect with a percentage of 26.2 and leadership-as-role at 17.6 percent, Leadership defined as a concept, as a phenomenon, and as a state were fifth, sixth, and seventh with percentages of 16.3, 14.2, and 11.3, respectively.

Seven percent of the 381 publications selected for *leadership* definition, interpretation, and classification were those of popular dictionaries from 1846 to 2004 (see the appendix, Table 4). Over 96 percent of the twenty-seven dictionaries classified were interpreted as publishing *leadership* defined as a role. *Leadership* defined as one or more characteristics was second in prevalence percentage with 77.8, followed by action at 63.0 percent; effect and state were fourth and fifth, respectively, with percentages of 11.1. The definitions of *leadership* from Simpson and Weiner (1989), the second edition of *The Oxford English Dictionary*, were categorized within four of the seven classifications: action, characteristic, effect, and role. None of the dictionaries defined *leadership* as either a concept or a phenomenon.

About 93 percent of the 381 publications selected for *leadership* definition interpretation and classification were those of nondictionary publications from 1902 to 2020 (see the appendix, Table 5). Over 70 percent of the 354 nondictionary publications classified were interpreted as publishing *leadership* defined as action. *Leadership* defined as one or more characteristics was a distant second in prevalence with 28.2 percent, followed by 27.4 percent of the publications defining *leadership* as an effect, 17.5 percent as a concept, 15.3 percent as a phenomenon, 11.6 percent as a role, and 11.3 percent as a state.

As a percentage of classifications of *leadership* defined as action, there was only a difference of 7.3 percent between nondictionary publications and those of popular dictionaries. The percentage of classification of *leadership* defined as a state by popular dictionaries was identical to nondictionary publications (see the appendix, Table 6). All of the rest of the percentage differences were significant, with popular-dictionary definitions being much more likely to define *leadership* as a role (96.3 percent) than nondictionary publications (11.6 percent) and as a characteristic (77.8) as compared to nondictionary publications (28.2 percent). Nondictionary publications were more likely to define *leadership* as a concept (17.5 percent) than popular dictionaries (0 percent), as an effect (27.4 percent compared to 11.1 percent), and as a phenomenon (15.3 percent compared to 0 percent).

Definitions of *leadership* published in popular dictionaries were also analyzed by time period. Because so few dictionaries were included for classification due to the selection criteria of popularity as determined after reviewing Steger (1913), Starnes and Noyes (1949), Green (1996), Landau (2001, 2009), and Bejoint (2010), classifications of definitions of *leadership* published in dictionaries were grouped within the fifty-four-year period of 1846–1899, the fifty-one-year period of 1900–1951, and the fifty-three-year period of 1952–2004 (see the appendix, Table 7).

The period of 1952–2004 returned the highest percentage of interpreted definitions of *leadership* in popular dictionaries that were categorized as defining it as a characteristic (100 percent) and as a role (100 percent). The period 1900–1951 returned a percentage of 100 for *leadership* defined as a role. *Leadership* defined as a characteristic returned a percentage of 83.3 for the period 1900–1951 and for period 1846–1899. The period 1952–2004 returned the highest percentage for the classification of action with 73.3 percent, followed by 66.7 percent for the period 1900–1951 and a percentage of 33.3 for the period 1846–1899. The period 1846–1899 returned 33.3 percent for *leadership* defined as a state among dictionaries selected for the study.

The remaining lower percentages of *leadership* definition classifications published in popular dictionaries were for the category of effect: 16.7 percent during the 1846–1899 period and 13.3 percent during the 1952–2004 period. Selected dictionaries that published a *leadership* definition classified as a definition of state returned a percentage of 6.7 during the period of 1952–2004. There were no definitions of leadership that were classified as a state during the period 1900–1951 or as a concept or phenomenon published in any of the dictionaries selected for this study.

Nondictionary publications presenting leadership definitions comprised the vast majority of works included within this study— nearly 93 percent. Ninety-six percent of the publications during the period 1970–1979 were interpreted to define *leadership* as action, and they are in order of highest percentage to lowest percentage by periods: 1990–1999, 2010–2020, 1980–1989, 2000–2009, 1940–1949, and 1950–1959 (see Table 8). The periods 1940–1949 and 1950–1959 returned the same percentage of definitions that described *leadership* as action. Only *leadership* defined as a characteristic during the periods 1900–1919 and 1930–1939 were among the top-ten preferences of authors. Clearly most nondictionary authors of leadership definitions moved away from describing *leadership* as a characteristic and preferred more often to define it as action beginning sometime in the 1940s. The period 1960–1969 returned the lowest percentage of leadership-as-action definitions after the period 1930–1939, but even then, *leadership* defined as action was still preferred by over half of the publications, with 53.6 percent of those publications defining *leadership* as action in the 1960–1969 period.

Leadership defined as one or more characteristics, after falling out of preference by authors dramatically during the 1940s and 1950s, seemed to experience a resurgence of popularity among authors and publications beginning in the 1960s, ranking in the top thirty of preference-rankings as a percentage of their definitions in the 1960s, 1970s, 1980s, and 2000s, and ranking in the top forty of percentage of preference-rankings during the 1990s and 2010s.

Leadership defined as an effect was proposed by many nondictionary authors, ranking in the top twenty of frequency-preference percentages during five of the eleven time periods analyzed: 1900–1919, 1920–1929, 1930–1939, 1950–1959, and 1960–1969. It was in the top thirty for 1980–1989 and 1990–1999 and the top forty for 1940–1949, 1970–1979, 2000–2009, and 2010–2020. Manager-centric definitions of *leadership* described *leadership* as group and organizational effectiveness and achievement, or a product of group interaction (Stogdill 1974; Bass 1981, 1990; Rost 1991, Bass and Bass 2008).

Leadership defined as a concept was preference-ranked by nondictionary authors as a percentage of all of their definitions by time period: once in the top twenty (1970–1979), once in the top thirty (1960–1969), and once in the top forty (1980–1989). Leadership-as-a-phenomenon was about the same as leadership-as-concept, with the period 1900–1919 returning one top-thirty preference-ranking by percentage, 1930–1939 returning one top-forty ranking, and the other nine time periods even lower in prevalence.

Leadership defined as a role or a state was the least preferred by nondictionary authors. Only once, during the period of 1900–1919, were *leadership* definitions interpreted as describing it as a role in the top thirty. *Leadership* defined as a state fared a little better with nondictionary authors, reaching the top twenty preferences once during the period 1940–1949, and reaching the top thirty during the period 1960–1969.

In summary, popular dictionaries selected for this study beginning with Worcester (1846) and going through Rooney and Soukhanov (2004), editors of the second edition of *Encarta Webster's Dictionary of the English Language*, were most likely to define *leadership* as a role expected to be performed by one or more people. *Leadership* defined as a role was consistent with leadership-as-a-role definitions authored by a minority of nondictionary authors interpreted in this study, consistent with the belief stated by French (1956) that leadership was dependent upon power of position referenced in popular textbooks today (Yukl and Gardner 2020; Northouse 2022). Nondictionary publications selected for this study, beginning with Cooley (1902) and going through Alvesson (2020); Fitzsimmons and Callan (2020); Garretsen, Stoker, and Weber (2020); Kelemen, Matthews, and Breevaart (2020); Pietraszewski (2020); and Waldman and O'Reilly (2020), were most likely to define *leadership* as action consistent with one of the four consolidated classifications of leader behavior of the twenty-one subclassifications of Bass and Bass (2008).

CHAPTER 5

A Definition of Leadership

THE GOAL OF this study was to develop a definition of leadership applicable to anyone—whether animal or human; owner, executive, manager, supervisor, subordinate, contractor, volunteer, customer, member of any organization, or a person independent of an organization; a politician or voter in any political nation, state, or locality; a parent or child; or a lover or friend in any social environment—that might prove beneficial to any reader. The goal of this study was to produce a definition of *leadership* with which most people would agree anywhere and at any time—a commonly accepted, context-free definition.

Stogdill (1974) believed a leadership definition should state who is a leader, how a leader acquired the position of leader, and how leadership is maintained. Bass (1990) departed from the belief of

Stogdill (1974) and Bass (1981) and stated a *leadership* definition should vary in accordance with different goals.

Rost (1991) seemed much more emphatic in his complaints about, and preferences and requirements for, a definition of *leadership* in complaining about the lack of clarity, conciseness, understandability, relevance, and persuasiveness of leadership definitions of practitioners and scholars in the past and advocated all of those criteria be included within a definition of the nature of leadership along with specificity, reality, and usefulness for making decisions. Bass and Bass (2008) stated a leadership definition should vary according to the leadership-definer's goal.

Steger (1913), a dictionary scholar, believed definitions should be brief, clear, and comprehensive. Landau (2001), a lexicographer and experienced editor-in-chief of dictionaries, included a brief history of definitions in communicating his criteria for definitions, which included both ancient and modern philosophers' views of definitional criteria, an explanation of different kinds of definitions (including logical definitions, which purport to define things that exist in reality, and lexical definitions, which classify things into categories and subcategories), and rules of definition and definitions of terms such as *definiendum*, the word being defined, and *definiens*, words that define definiendums.

Included among the common rules of lexicography are that definitions should attempt to express definitions positively as opposed to negatively, that definitions should attempt to define the nature of things as those things exist in reality, and that none of the words of definiens should be any form of the definiendum (Landau 2001), a rule that so many leadership scholars and practitioners break when they used the words *lead, leading,* or *leader* within their definition of *leadership*. It appears, though, nearly all leadership writers who have defined *leadership* in print have attempted to capture the essence of leadership, with only a very small number defining leadership by explaining what leadership is not.

Another rule of definitions, which was cited as being presented by Zgusta originally, was that every word of a definition should exist in the same tense as the definiendum and that every word used to define a definiendum should be explained and defined in its own right, as if the person reading the definition for the first time has no knowledge whatsoever of the definiendum (Landau 2001). That way, clarity is ensured and misunderstanding is avoided. Simplicity, brevity, and clarity should be the goals of definition-writing.

Bejoint (2010) echoed the rules and recommendations of Landau (2001), stressing the need for definitions to be simple, avoid circularity of defining words by a form of the same word, use stand-alone words in definiens, and use words in definiens that are not limited by context—a rule which some leadership-definers have violated by defining *leadership* as existing when a certain situation or circumstance exists.

Kort (2008), a philosopher who published a definition of leadership (see Table 1 in the appendix), referenced two philosophers, Patrick Hurley and Lori Watson. In their thirteenth edition, Hurley and Watson (2018) defined and explained the different kinds of definitions: lexical, which states the way words are used in language (such as definitions in dictionaries); precising, which attempts to decrease ambiguity of definiendums used so prevalently in the legal system; theoretical, which states interpretations of a phenomenon or phenomena; and persuasive, which uses words designed to sway the opinions or feelings of readers or listeners.

In accordance with some of the rules of definition prescribed by Steger (1913), Landau (2001), Bejoint (2010), and Rost (1991) of brevity, clarity, and understandability, Grint (2010a, 2) observed, "Without followers you cannot be a leader. Indeed, this might be the simplest definition of leadership: 'having followers,'" which seemed to be a good starting point for the development of an attempted context-free, commonly accepted definition of *leadership*. Researching all of the words related most closely to *leadership*, which include *follower, follow, following, followership, leader, lead,* and *leading,* was not part of the review of literature, even though reviewing dictionaries beginning with Cawdrey (1604) to find the earliest definitions of *leadership* did yield definitions of other leadership-related words with the exception of the word *followership,* seemingly the latest addition to dictionaries of the seven words most closely connected to *leadership.*

The word *having* in the present tense, as defined by popular dictionaries from 1922 to 2018, means possessing something (Vizetelly 1922; Friend and Guralnik, 1953; Gove 1961; Barnhart 1963; Gove 1963; Costello 1991/1992; Mish 1993/1994, 2003/2014; Pickett, 2011/2018; Kleinedler 2014/2018, 2016). The idea of possession seems incongruent with leadership.

The word *followers* seems closer to the mark in the way of accuracy, but it is the plural form of the word *follower.* More than one follower was not required in the approach to leadership of Dansereau, Graen, and Haga (1975), who viewed leadership as a relationship between an organizational manager and a subordinate in which exchange occurred between the two. In the same year, Graen and Cashman (1975, 146) termed the same relationship "Leader-Member Exchange," which Graen, Novak, and Sommerkamp (1982, 109) shortened to "LMX." Both of those publications were descriptive in nature whereas Graen and Uhl-Bien (1995) reported the stages of development of LMX and offered a prescriptive version of what managers should do as opposed to the nature of exchanges that develop between managers and subordinates. Northouse (2022), the most popular textbook in the world, reported LMX is still supported in the leadership literature of today because LMX has produced organizational benefits in terms of lower turnover and increased productivity, however productivity was defined. Yukl and Gardner (2020), in their review of LMX, reported a similar positive benefit regarding increased task accomplishment.

The popular definition of leadership of Hersey and Blanchard (1972) and their most recent tenth edition of Hersey, Blanchard, and Johnson (2013) in their textbook as well as the third edition of Antonakis and Day (2018) stated that *leadership* could include only one follower. However, other authors of popular textbooks have stated that *leadership* does not exist if there is one follower only (Rost 1991; Northouse 1997, 2022). However, no apparent logical reason could be found to support the claim that *leadership* requires more than one follower and cannot exist in respect to a parent and one child, a teacher and one student, a lover or friend and another lover or friend, a therapist, doctor, or counselor and one patient or client, a sales representative and one customer, and an organizational manager and one subordinate. One follower can create and maintain *leadership*.

A number of authors who defined *leadership* and were included within this study posed the question "What is leadership?" in various ways, either in the title or within the main body of text (Vroom and Jago 2007; Kort 2008; Springborg 2010; Silva 2016; Grint, Smolovic Jones, and Holt 2016). According to popular dictionaries published during the past century, the word *leadership* is formed by adding the suffix of *-ship* to the base word of *leader*, which possesses the suffix *-er*, the noun form of the verb *lead* (Vizetelly 1922; Friend and Guralnik 1953; Gove 1961, 1963; Barnhart 1963; Costello 1991/1992; Mish 1993/1994, 2003/2014; Pickett 2011/2018; Kleinedler 2014/2018, 2016). Therefore, the essential elements of a definition of leadership should include words that are consistent with the words *leader* and *lead*. Logically, one leads in the present tense and was or is a leader in the past and present tenses. One can neither lead in the past nor lead in the future. Likewise, one cannot be a leader in the future.

As stated previously, the purpose of this study was to find and analyze definitions of *leadership* as a means to proposing a commonly accepted, universally applicable definition. It seemed logical to define the word *what* as a means of determining a definition of *leadership* despite the fact some leadership definitions found and analyzed included the interrogatives when, where, why, and how, in addition to communicating what leadership is and who, if anyone, was included within the definition. Former newspaper reporter and editor, professor emeritus, and author of a number of publications in news media Stovall (2005, 153) observed that journalism reporters attempt to "answer six basic questions for the reader: Who … What … When … Where … Why and how."

According to the most popular dictionaries published during the past century, the word *what* refers to the essential nature of something in existence (Vizetelly 1922; Friend and Guralnik 1953; Gove 1961, 1963; Barnhart 1963; Costello 1991/1992; Mish 1993/1994, 2003/2014; Pickett 2011/2018; Kleinedler 2014/2018, 2016). The word *who* refers to the identity of someone.

In the general public, the word *leadership* is used in multiple ways.

For example, the phrase "he or she brings leadership to the team" implies a definition of *leadership* as an ability, capacity, potential, or some other similar characterization. The use of the phrase "the leadership of the organization" implies a definition of *leadership* as a person or group of people. The use of the phrase "that was leadership" can imply a definition of *leadership* as a past result that is viewed as a benefit, consistent with the definer's value system of morality (the degree to which one helps oneself and others and avoids harming oneself and others) and effectiveness (the degree to which one accomplishes one's goals and helps another accomplish the other's goals).

People respond to events that take place during the time periods in which they live. During US involvement in the Vietnam War of the 1960s and early 1970s and the US Watergate scandal (1972–1974), Greenleaf (1972, 1973) published the earliest versions of servant leadership, which included the element of giving support for ethical behavior within his definition of *leadership* in 1972 (see Table 1). Servant leadership has become more popular since the early 1970s, and so have other morality-based popular leadership approaches such as authentic and ethical leadership (Northouse 2022).

Burns (1976) referenced the Watergate scandal nearly twenty times in the book he published before Burns (1978/1979), within which he presented transforming leadership, stating, "Transforming leaders 'raise' their followers up through levels of morality" (426). Burns devoted an entire chapter to moral leadership. Many people have been called leaders politically and organizationally, including the famous Adolph Hitler before and during World War II. An American political scientist, Burns (1978/1979) stated "Hitler, once he gained power and crushed all opposition, was no leader—he was a tyrant" (2–3), "an absolute wielder of brutal power" (27), but on other pages, Burns stated Hitler was one among "great leaders" (58) or a "great leader" (285), a "remote leader" of German soldiers (292), and one of the "global leaders" along with Franklin Roosevelt of the United States, Joseph Stalin of Russia, and Mohandas (Mohatma) Gandhi of India (302). The use of the qualifier "once he gained power" (2–3) could be interpreted to mean Burns, who defined power as "a *relationship* among persons" within which "power holders (P) … have the capacity to secure change in the behavior of a respondent (R), human or animal, and in the environment" (12–13), may have thought Hitler was a leader before he gained the chancellorship in 1933 or dictatorship in 1934, although no clear line of demarcation was found in terms of which exact year was meant.

Hitler was followed by a significant percentage of Germans in the beginning (Childers 1984; Hamilton 1986; Saunders 2003; Parsons 2007; Ferguson 2008; King, Rosen, Tanner, and Wagner 2008; Koehne 2013; Goeschel 2017; Satyanath, Voigtlaender, and Voth, 2017; Spenkuch and Tillman, 2018; Voigtlaender and Voth, 2019). All of the people and organizations that supported Hitler endorsed him because it was believed to be in their self-interest to do so. As Germany's defeats and losses in World War II began to mount, however, Hitler lost the support of those that once followed him.

McClelland (1975) was referenced by Burns (1978/1979) in his definition of power wielders like Hitler and stated, "The motives of power wielders may or may not coincide with what the respondent wants done … and if they must make a choice between satisfying their own purposes and satisfying respondents' needs, they will choose the former" (14–15). In a political journal article devoted solely to the psychology of individuals who possess the power to commit their nation-states to a certain course of action internally, McClelland (1970) labeled Lenin of Russia and Hitler of Germany "great demagogues" who "established their power over the masses which followed loyally and obediently" (37), describing the environment in both of those countries at the time those power wielders ruled as "the 'law of the jungle' in which the strongest survive by destroying their adversaries" (36).

Hitler (1925/1939) himself, in his own definition of leadership, included the word "adversary" (see Table 1). The motives of those characterized as possessing personalized power as defined by McClelland (1970) were supported by studies reported in McClelland (1985) and referenced by Howell (1988) in her characterization of Hitler as one who used followers to achieve his own goals. Howell and Avolio (1992) labeled Hitler as one of the "unethical charismatic leaders" along with many CEOs of major corporations (51). In the same publication within which Burns (1998) described Hitler as a "non-leader" (xii) and "the most universally detested man in history" (ix), Bass (1998) stated Hitler was a "pseudotransformational leader" (171), a term still used in the characterization of Hitler to this day (Northouse 2022).

The fact remains that no matter whether one defines leadership morally or morality-free, leadership includes the word *leader*, one that leads. Therefore, it is logical to assume a common definition of *leadership* should include, at minimum, a word or words that indicate who is in included within the definition and what leadership is.

Stogdill (1974, 274) observed the difficulty of measuring leadership because "the range of possible combinations of variables is very large." This seems to be the problem with leadership measures in general. If one is proposing theories of how to lead, it is very probable there are too many potential leader behaviors and characteristics to measure.

Yukl and Gardner (2020) listed many measures of leadership used by researchers in the past, which included "follower dissatisfaction and hostility toward the leader" such as "absenteeism, voluntary turnover" (8). Buckingham and Coffman (1999), in their report of results of a study conducted in four hundred companies by the Gallup Organization, claimed, "An employee may *join* Disney or GE or Time Warner because she is lured by their generous benefits package and their reputation for valuing employees. But it is her relationship with her immediate manger that will determine *how long she stays* and *how productive* she is while she is there" (36).

As a means of formulating a definition of leadership, it seems logical to arrive at a reason why people and animals follow. Kellerman (2008) answered that question with "self-interest ... the benefits of following outweigh those of not following ... consciously or unconsciously" (49, 55). Years later, to bolster her point, Kellerman (2019) wrote about an exercise she conducted to raise the consciousness of "supporters" of US president Donald Trump's words, actions, and representations by having them self-divide themselves into "true believers" and those who "concluded that it was in their interest to remain in a relationship with him" (45). Agreement with another's words, action, or representation is a matter of degree on a continuum of agreement and disagreement. Agreement with another's words, action, or representation determines whether one is following.

Voting behavior, approval rating, and presidential administration turnover are measures of following. Following in relation to political organizational leadership of US presidents can be measured in various ways, but three ways are by reelection, approval rating as determined by reputable polls, and turnover of employees. In national and statewide elections held in the United States, people follow political ideology and political parties in addition to individual candidates.

In the US presidential elections of 2004 and 2008, about 90 percent of voters reported voting for their political party's candidate (Caraley 2009). Only 7 percent of Americans polled don't "lean" toward either the Republican Party or the Democratic Party (Laloggia 2019). Most local elections and some judicial elections are nonpartisan (Northup 1987) and result in lower voter turnout (Schaffner, Streb, and Wright, 2001; Lim and Snyder 2012), but most people vote for candidates of only one party in both national and statewide elections instead of voting for candidates representing another party or an independent with no party affiliation (Magleby, Nelson, and Westlye 2011; Rakich and Best 2020).

Beginning with Franklin Roosevelt's election in 1932, of the ten US presidents who were popularly elected to a first term of office, only three have failed to win reelection: James Carter in 1980, George H. W. Bush in 1992, and Donald Trump in 2020.

Jones (2021) reported the highest average job-approval rating of a US president by those Americans polled by Gallup beginning with Harry Truman, who took office in 1945, was the 70 percent average approval of John Kennedy, who served less than three years of his four-year term. The president with the highest average rating of those who served all eight years of their two terms was Dwight Eisenhower, with 65 percent. Of those presidents who served only four years due to defeat in their reelection bid, George H. W. Bush polled the highest with an approval rating of 61 percent, and Donald Trump polled the lowest with an average job-approval rating of 41 percent. Never once did Trump achieve a 50 percent job-approval rating in any poll conducted by Gallup during his four years in office.

Another measure of following in political organizational leadership is retention as measured by its inverse, turnover. Tenpas (2021) compared turnover of "senior-ranking advisors in the executive office of the president" and cabinet members in five presidential administrations from 1981 to 2021. The two Bush administrations had the lowest turnover rates of senior advisors, and George W. Bush had the lowest turnover of cabinet members. The Trump administration had the highest turnover of both senior advisors and cabinet members.

Turnover and turnover intention of individuals (which has been found to correlate with turnover) has been linked to leadership ineffectiveness and reported to support popular theories of leadership such as leader-member exchange (LMX) (Graen, Novak, and Sommerkamp 1982; Dulebohn, Bommer, Liden, Brouer, and Ferris 2012), transformational leadership (Tse, Huang, and Lam 2013; Waldman, Carter, and Hom, 2015), and empowering leadership (Chen, Sharma, Edinger, Shapiro, and Farh, 2011; Kim and Beehr 2020).

Organizations follow other organizations, in an attempt to prosper and survive against competition locally, nationally, and internationally. Nation-states compete against other countries by adopting policies and regulations that attempt to maximize the strengths and minimize the weaknesses of their organizations, which are competing in other countries within various industries. For example, according to Magaziner and Hout (1980), Japanese auto manufacturers, aided by industrial policies of Japan, began competing successfully in the US automobile industry in the 1970s, which caused American officials to consider change within their industry and to travel to Japan to learn how its government was working with and supporting industries there. In the wake of the 1981–1982 US recession, President Ronald Reagan established a Commission on Industrial Competitiveness in 1983 to advise him so his administration could help US industries "compete in the international marketplace" (Reagan 1983b).

Michael Porter was appointed to Reagan's Commission on Industrial Competitiveness (Reagan 1983a). Porter (1980) presented a model of competitive strategy that individual organizations could implement to compete within various industries both locally and nationally. Later, Porter (1985) further explained how an individual organizational firm described as a "follower" in a certain industry could follow an organization, which was termed a "market leader from the perspective of followers," and how all organizations could identify and improve their competitiveness (216). Porter (1990) addressed international competition specifically. Nation-states follow other nation-states. Some nation-states are leaders in certain ways while other nation-states follow those leaders.

In addition to political parties, governments, and businesses, other organizations are followed: nonprofits such as nongovernmental organizations (NGOs), special interest groups, activist organizations, trade unions, religious denominations, and churches, among many others. No matter the type of organization, joining an organization is an indicator of following. Leaving an organization is a measure of not following. When people seek employment or volunteer to be managed by supervisors of organizations at various levels within the organizational hierarchy without having recent and direct experience with the supervisor or organization previously, they decide which organizations to follow based on information they possess at the time.

The secondhand, hearsay information prospective employees and volunteers possess at the time of their decision to join organizations is based on representations of organizations, which have been labeled by authors such as Cable and Yu (2006) as "organizational images ... an audience's beliefs about the traits ... about the company," which "help people differentiate a firm from competitors" (828). Bromley (1993) observed "things ... said or believed about people and things vary from ... unanimous agreement ... to ... only one person's agreement" and stated, "Beliefs can remain unspoken," don't necessarily "correspond to the truth," and may not be expressed honestly (1) in relation to public corporate image reputations formed, which can consist of a "particular characteristic—of having done something, of being able to do something, or having some outstanding attribute" (2).

The same process that was detailed previously in chapter 2 to describe how the seven leadership definition classifications of action, characteristic, concept, effect, phenomenon, role, and state were determined in this study was used again in consulting the same popular dictionaries spanning nearly one hundred years to determine whether the definition of the word *representation* was supported from a lexicographic point of view. All of the definitions of *representation* published in popular dictionaries from 1922 to 2018 stated *representation* stood for something or someone else in potential form of a likeness, an image, a symbol, or something similar to the actual person or thing represented (Vizetelly 1922; Friend and Guralnik 1953; Gove 1961, 1963; Barnhart 1963; Costello 1991/1992;

Mish 1993/1994, 2003/2014; Pickett 2011/2018; Kleinedler 2014/2018, 2016).

People and organizations are either represented or misrepresented on a continuum of accuracy ranging from an exact duplicate or copy on one end to an incompetent falsehood or conscious lie on the other end. If people make decisions to follow or not follow someone or something else based on accurate representations of others, they are more likely to continue to follow. If people feel betrayed by misrepresentations of others, they are less likely to follow dependent upon the degree of choice they believe they possess.

Of all of the theories, models, and approaches to leadership, path-goal leadership theory began taking into account the motivation of those whose supervisors attempt to lead in the 1970s. House (1971) presented the theory initially. Another version followed in the same decade (House and Mitchell 1974) and an even more complex version over twenty years later was published in House (1996).

In an attempt to discover ways of enhancing organizational productivity, Georgopoulos, Mahoney, and Jones (1957, 345) of the University of Michigan's Survey Research Center proposed a "path-goal approach" of motivation, upon which Vroom (1964) based in part his expectancy concept. Evans (1970, 279) based his "path-goal instrumentality" motivation theory upon both Georgopoulos, Mahoney, and Jones (1957) and Vroom (1964). Although most of the people associated with the Survey Research Center at the University of Michigan, which sponsored Georgopoulos, Mahoney, and Jones (1957), are deceased, Jack French, as he was nicknamed, authored a theory of social power in French (1956) and may have been the person who coined the term *path-goal*, according to Arnold Tannenbaum, a research scientist at the Survey Research Center at the time (A. Tannenbaum, personal communication, April 25, 2020).

In the same year Evans (1996) suggested path-goal theory needed to be reevaluated, House (1996) revised his earlier versions of path-goal theory by proposing ten different classifications of different behaviors a manager could implement that would be effective with and for organizational subordinates, which amounted to five path-goal clarifying behaviors, one achievement-oriented behavior, thirteen work-facilitation behaviors, one supportive behavior, five interaction-facilitation behaviors, eight group-oriented decision-process behaviors, ten representation-and-networking behaviors, and twelve value-based leader behaviors, all of which could be performed by non-formally-appointed personnel. The sheer volume and complexity associated with the new, modified version of path-goal theory is overwhelming.

All of the versions of path-goal theory have led a significant number of publications to label path-goal theory as complex and difficult to interpret (Yukl and Gardner 2020; Northouse 2022). During the period 2000–2012, according to Dinh, Lord, Gardner, Meuser, Liden, and Hu (2014), articles devoted to path-goal theory published in leadership scholarly journals amounted to 1 percent. During the period 2013–2019, Gardner, Lowe, Meuser, Noghani, Gullifor, and Cogliser (2020) reported no articles devoted to path-goal theory published in *The Leadership Quarterly*, the flagship of leadership scholarly journals.

Cote (2017) questioned the existence of a link between one's impact on another's motivation in accordance with the theory of expectancy upon which the path-goal theory of House and Mitchell (1974) and the modifications of path-goal theory published in House

(1996) were based. Cullen (2015) criticized the validity of path-goal theory because of research results that varied too much from the theory in terms of being effective, because of task complexity, and because of apparent misunderstanding of human motivation in the workplace in relation to work-value variation from individual to individual. Valuing goals differently varies by individual based on their own personal values. The number of personal values of those who choose to follow are not only voluminous; many are unconscious. If the person making the decision to follow or not follow, no matter how following is defined, is unaware of why he or she is following, how can a theory of leadership prescribe all of the possible behaviors that might be effective in acquiring and maintaining followership—if accomplishment of that objective is even possible? Everyone can't be led at all times.

Path-goal theory is dead, but the earliest foundation for it, published in Georgopoulos, Mahoney, and Jones (1957), is as alive now as it was in the mid-twentieth century and will continue to live so long as organisms exist. People and animals follow based on their decisions to follow no matter whether their motivations are based on values, instinct, or learned response.

A subordinate employee or volunteer of an organization follows an organization if he or she stays with the organization due to the benefits of retaining the leadership of the organization. The same employee or volunteer follows a person if the employee or volunteer stays with the organization due to the benefits of retaining the leadership of his or her supervisor, or in the case of some organizations, multiple supervisors. If the same followed leader leaves the organization for another organization, and the employee or volunteer leaves the organization to follow the leader to the new organization, the employee or organization has followed his or her leader.

Nations, organizations, voters, prospective and current members of organizations, and others follow. The self-interest Kellerman (2008) offered as a reason why people follow those who are admired for their position and their behavior even if they do not agree with everything they do, is based on values.

Burns (1978/1979, 43) cited "modal values" and "end-values" of Rokeach (1973) in support of the case he made for the morality-increase potential of leadership. In addition to Burns (1978/1979), which cited some values discovered and published by Rokeach (1973), Bass (1981) advocated followers need to become aware of their internal psychological conflicts and cited Rokeach (1971), which reported a procedure that enabled people to accomplish that very objective. Later, Bass and Bass (2008) quoted the value definition of Rokeach (1973) and paraphrased other information.

Rokeach (1973) defined a value as "an enduring belief that a specific mode of conduct or end-state of existence is personally or socially preferrable to an opposite or converse mode of conduct or end-state of existence" and a value system as "an enduring organization of beliefs concerning preferable modes of conduct or end-states of existence along a continuum of relative importance" (5).

Other concepts of personal values related to those of organizational managers was reported in publications such as England, Dhingra, and Agarwal (1974) and the well-known motivational theory of Maslow (1943), which proposed "Human needs arrange themselves in hierarchies of prepotency" (370) and continues to be cited in popular textbooks such as Robbins and Coulter (2018) and Daft (2018) as a theory of motivation even though it has failed validation in several studies (Soper, Milford, and Rosenthal 1995; Wahba and Bridwell 1976; Lawler and Suttle 1972).

The benefits-versus-costs calculation people make in their decisions to follow or not follow, stated by Kellerman (2008), may have roots within the exchange theory of Thibaut and Kelley (1959), who proposed that people who interact with others attempt to achieve some "immediate goal or end state" (10–11), the result of which amounts to the "rewards a person receives and the costs he incurs" (12). In other words, people behave in the best interests of themselves either consciously or unconsciously to maintain their value systems and make conscious or unconscious choices in their lives based on the potential rewards they can maintain or acquire while attempting to minimize the costs they might suffer as a consequence of their choices. People are constantly making choices on what to do or not do, either consciously or unconsciously.

People and organizations that follow other people and organizations are not static because the value systems of people and organizations are not static. People and organizations change to whichever degree and pace.

Values are the ethical and effective principles people and organizations live by and the long-term goals they seek. Values are conscious or unconscious and exist in different degrees of importance within people as habits and within organizations as culture. Organizational culture was defined in Deal and Kennedy (1982, 4) by McKinsey and Company management consultant Marvin Bower as "the way we do things around here." Schein (1985, 15) observed that people learn culture, which is "someone's original values ... of what 'ought' to be, as distinct from what is."

Just as there is no consensus on the definition of leadership,

Rokeach (1968) made the same observation about the definition of "a belief ... a value," and a "value system" (x) but defined a belief as a "proposition, conscious or unconscious, inferred from what a person says or does, capable of being preceded by the phrase 'I believe that ...' The content of a belief may describe the object of belief as true or false, correct or incorrect; evaluate it as good or bad; or advocate a certain course of action or a state of existence as desirable or undesirable" (113), a belief system as "the total ... of a person's beliefs about the physical world, the social world, and the self" (123), a value as a "type of belief ... about how one ought or ought not to behave, or about some end-state of existence worth or not worth attaining," and a value system as a "hierarchical organization—a rank ordering—of ideals or values in terms of importance" (124–125).

People, animals, and organizations follow other individuals and organizations because they agree with other individuals, ideologies, or organizations in some way. Some species of animals follow because it is in their self-interest to do so in order to adapt and survive in their environment (Van Vugt 2006; Van Vugt, Hogan, and Kaiser 2008). For people, agreement that causes them to follow is based on beliefs and values. As Rousseau (1995, 6) observed, "Agreement exists in the eye of the beholder." The word *follow* in the present tense, as defined by popular dictionaries within the last century applicable to *leadership*, means to do something after and similar in some way to someone or something else (Vizetelly 1922; Friend and Guralnik 1953; Gove 1961, 1963; Barnhart 1963; Costello 1991/1992; Mish 1993/1994, 2003/2014; Pickett 2011/2018; Kleinedler 2014/2018, 2016).

Although the goal of this research was to locate and analyze multiple definitions of leadership in an attempt to determine a common definition of leadership, definitions of *following, follower, followership, leading,* and *leader* are included as a basis of foundation. *To follow* and *to lead* are both infinitive forms of *follow* and *lead*. *Following* and *leading* are both formed by adding the suffix *-ing*, which emphasize the verbs *follow* and *lead*, both present states of action.

It is appropriate to determine who is defining a term in terms of his or her status and in relation to the terms being defined. Within the framework of following, it is assumed a person, animal, or organization is either a follower or a nonfollower. Also, it is assumed both animals and people decide to follow or not follow another to accomplish their own objectives, which is (in the case of animals) to accomplish the goal of survival. People attempt to accomplish goals by following another, but in addition they employ values and value systems to decide which goals to attempt to accomplish (Rokeach 1973).

People who decline to follow another make their decision not to follow based on their belief the other's action, words, result, or representation will not provide means for the accomplishment of their personal goals. Means are defined as anything that can facilitate goal accomplishment. In other words, and as harsh as it may seem, all leaders are, to followers, means to desired ends. Animals and people desire to survive physiologically. People desire to survive psychologically as well.

As a means of surviving based on values and value systems, people are capable of imagining desired future states of existence and take action to realize those future states. People follow another because it is believed the other will facilitate the person's goal of achieving some desired future state of existence. Therefore, it is assumed people who choose to decline to follow another make that choice based on the belief the other will not provide the means to accomplish some valued personal goal.

The transforming leadership in Burns (1978/1979) is altruistic in part in that it states levels of "morality" is increased (20). Punj and Krishnan (2006) referenced publications that stated transformational leadership helps others to think of others more as opposed to themselves and found support for a link of transformational leadership to altruism on the part of followers in a study of over one hundred managers and subordinates in India. However, the definitions of *follow*, *following*, *follower*, *followership*, *lead*, *leading*, *leader*, and *leadership* stated in this chapter assume that leaders exist as a means to others' goals and that altruism, defined as attempting to provide a benefit to another without conscious or unconscious self-interest, does not exist.

Some authors have proposed leadership is coproduced in follower-centric ways and is a process implemented by one that intends to lead and others that intend to follow (Shamir 2007; Carsten and Uhl-Bien 2012; Carsten, Harmes, and Uhl-Bien 2014). A series of intentional steps to lead another can occur before another has decided to follow, which can result in and maintain a state of leadership, but the state of leadership does not exist initially in all circumstances and environments.

Politically and within situations wherein individuals have little or no knowledge of each other, a more accurate verb than *coproduce* in definition of how leadership occurs within some contexts is the word *discover*. In some cases, individuals discovering another can provide the means for goal accomplishment and decide to follow whether the one leading is aware of being followed or not. Animals, people, and organizations follow to accomplish the goals of the animals, people, and organizations that are following. Animals, people, and organizations lead if another is following. To follow is to emulate or express agreement with another's words, action, or representation.

Following is emulating another or expressing agreement with another's words, action, or representation. Emulating is acting or communicating in the same manner as another is acting or communicating or has acted or communicated in the past. Another is anyone or anything separate from the one that is emulating. Acting in the same manner is doing something identical or similar to the actions of another. Communicating in the same manner is sending a message to another that is identical or similar to communications sent by another. Emulating exists in the present on a continuum that ranges from similarity to sameness. Similarity means something more like something else than different. Sameness means being identical.

Expressing is acting. Acting is doing something. Agreement is being in accord. Accord is being in harmony with another. Words are elements of language. A representation is anything that stands in place of action or words of another. Agreement exists in the present on a continuum that ranges from hope to belief. Hope is an expectation something is more likely to be true or real than not. Belief is a more certain faith and trust something truthfully exists.

To lead is to be emulated or agreed with by another. Leading is being emulated by or agreed with by another. A follower is one that is emulating or expressing agreement with another's action, words, or representation. A leader is one that is being emulated or agreed with by another.

Followership is a state of emulation of or agreement with another's action, words, or representation. A state is the existence of something at some time. Leadership is a state of being emulated or agreed with by another.

A state exists at a point in time. There are many states of being. A relationship is a state of connection. A state of leadership exists at a point in time. A state of leadership can exist for seconds, whereas leading is occurring in the present, or a state of leadership can exist over time while leading is not occurring. A state of leadership is transitory. A state of leadership can cease to exist in one or more seconds when the one that is following or is in a state of followership has decided to terminate the state.

Followers determine leadership with their behavior, thoughts, and feelings. Nonfollowers define leadership based upon their beliefs of what leadership is whether they believe it is behavior, ability, an effect, a position, or a state. Although followers may be less conscious of their emulating of or state of emulation of another, followers are more likely to know whether or not they are agreeing with or believing in another as opposed to merely complying with another for the purpose of survival at a lower level of existence. Followers are the best definers of leadership with their behavior, thoughts, and feelings as opposed to nonfollowers, who are defining leadership in their own best interests, whatever those interests are.

Most organizational managers and individuals acquire information on the subject of leadership to achieve their own personal goals. A CEO or other organizational manager who hires a firm or an individual, purchases publications, views virtual presentations, or takes other actions to improve leadership assumes improving leadership will be the means to increased organizational effectiveness, efficiency, or both. Individuals who are not in a position of organizational authority and organizational executives, managers, or supervisors who want to improve their effectiveness in their personal lives interacting with another acquire information about leadership no matter how it is labeled.

Very few people in the United States acquire information on how to follow, although the followership market for information seems to be increasing. Following is emulating or agreeing at minimum. Most managers and individuals without organizational authority who want improvement, no matter how they define improvement, want that improvement for the sake of accomplishing goals. However, people follow other individuals, managers, and organizations as a means to accomplishing the personal goals of those choosing to follow. The most certain way to accomplish leadership is to gain the agreement of those whom one attempts to lead.

Always there is a conflict between the goals of the organization as determined by those at the highest levels of organizational authority and the goals of everyone else in the organization. Public corporations experience conflict at times between stockholders, boards of directors, executives, managers, supervisors, and those who report to them who do not have supervisory responsibility. In organizations, always there will be conflict between the values and goals of the organization as a whole and the values and goals of those who are attempting to achieve their own personal goals.

Everyone can't be led. The person who believes or states he or she can lead any other is either delusional, hasn't attempted to lead a significant number of others in a multitude of environments, or possesses a definition of leadership that is either nonexistent or dissimilar to most mainstream definitions of *lead*, *follow*, and the respective suffixes of those two words.

Emulation may not be perceived as being as important as

agreement, but words that indicate one will do what another does is communicated and believed because people do respond favorably to exemplary behavior by the one attempting to lead. However, if the exemplary behavior is not consistent with the values and goals of the individual one is attempting to lead, behavior will not be emulated.

Agreement is the minimum of leading, being a leader, or leadership. Many definitions, approaches, models, and theories of leadership state how to lead. Complexity is the problem with including the interrogatives of how, why, when, and where within definitions of *follow*, *lead*, and their suffixes. People are too dissimilar. The path-goal theory of House (1996) includes fifty-five potential actions of those defined as leading in the accomplishment of leadership. The ways people can and will respond to each one of the fifty-five different stimuli must number in the hundreds if not thousands.

Agreement is achieved by learning the personal values and goals of each one of the people whom one desires to lead. Learning the personal values and goals of people takes time. Everyone is different to whichever degree.

Phrases heard by those attempting to facilitate leadership and followership in others include "That's not my job" "I don't have time," "I can't do that," "That won't work," and others of similar ilk. *Can't* and *won't* never accomplished anything.

Some people don't want to communicate personal values and goals, but the end-state of agreement should be reached as a minimum of leadership and one believed capable of facilitating personal goal accomplishment as a maximum. Ideally, attempting to lead should never end, although sometimes the states of followership and leadership cannot be achieved because the goals of the organization must take precedence.

Some people will choose to leave the organization because their personal values and goals cannot be realized. Some people will choose to stay with the organization and cause conflict. However, the more agreement is reached, the less conflict should result.

Conflict can be minimized if the person one is attempting to lead believes that the manager is doing everything possible to accomplish the person's goals and agrees with the manager's plan to facilitate goal accomplishment or agrees the manager cannot facilitate goal accomplishment either immediately or in the long term. Consistent with many approaches and models of moralistic leadership, agreement, and belief is best served by communicating what is believed to be accurate at the time of communication.

Sometimes one is powerless to help another accomplish a goal, but that too should be communicated by the manager. Power is what another fears or wants. The power to acquire and maintain followership can be great if a manager helps another accomplish what he or she wants either consciously or unconsciously.

Agreement is the minimum, but belief is the gold standard. If one believes another is doing all he or she can to facilitate one's goal accomplishment, the likelihood of leadership and followership is greatest.

APPENDIX

Table 1. Dictionary and Nondictionary Definitions
of What Leadership Is and Contexts, Interpretations,
and Classifications of Definitions

Publication Citation	Definitions and Contexts	Classification
Allport 1924/1964, 419–420	"Leadership … means the direct, face-to-face contact between leader and followers: it is personal social control … the phenomenon of control of the followers by the leader … The process."	Action, Effect, Phenomenon
Alvesson 2020, 10	"Leadership is interaction."	Action
Alvesson and Spicer 2014, 42–43	"Leadership involves … meaning management … in which the shaping of the ideas, values, perceptions and feelings is central … the management of meaning … can be very much about maintaining, revising, or strengthening ideas, beliefs, morale, values … understandings … can also involve coercive elements … legitimately enacted … a system of norms encouraging respect and compliance with authority figures … a feeling that the leader (or others in the environment) … can create problems for those not receptive … power element."	Action, Effect, Role
Andersen 2014, 95, 99	"Leadership … is a function performed by managers as well as by informal leaders."	Role

Andriessen and Drenth 1984, 483	"The concept leadership: *Leadership is that part of the role of a (appointed or elected) leader that in interaction with the group is directly linked to influencing the behaviour of the group, or the behaviour of one or more members of the group and is expressed through directing and coordinating activities that are important in connection with the tasks of the group (in the organization)."*	Concept, Role
Antonakis and Atwater 2002, 676	"Leadership is an influencing process that results from follower perceptions of leader behavior and follower attributions of leader dispositional characteristics, behavior, and performance."	Action
Antonakis, Cianciolo, and Sternberg 2004, 5	"Leadership can be defined as the nature of the influencing process— and its resultant outcomes—that occurs between a leader and followers and how this influencing process is explained by the leader's dispositional characteristics and behaviors, follower perceptions and attributions of the leader, and the context in which the influencing process occurs."	Action, Concept, Effect
Antonakis and Day 2018, 5	"Leadership is a formal or informal contextually rooted and goal-influencing process that occurs between a leader and a follower, groups of followers, or institutions."	Action
Arvey, Wang, Song, and Li 2014, 73	"'Leadership' … signifying one person exerting influence on followers to achieve certain kind of goals … also … leadership is sometimes viewed as role-inherent … people in formal management roles … are also considered 'leaders' by … power and authority … in 'leadership positions.'"	Effect, Role

Ashford and DeRue 2012, 146	"Leadership is … influencing people and processes in service of a collective aim or goal."	Effect
Atwater and Yammarino 1992, 145, 147	"Leadership (abilities and experiences)."	Characteristic
Avolio 2007, 31	"Leadership is a function of both the leader and the led and the complexity of the context."	Action, Effect
Baker 2006, 18	"Leadership: a process by which a person fills the role of leader influencing another or others to achieve goals held in common with the leader or organization."	Action
Baker, Anthony, and Stites-Doe 2015, 28–29	"Leadership is both a process and an outcome."	Action, Effect
Baliga and Hunt, J. C. 1988, 129–130	"Leadership within the context of organizationally-derived managerial tasks … Instances in which organizational members create and exercise discretion in tasks that have limited or no discretionary elements … the leadership component of managerial roles."	Action, Role
Bann 2007, 15	"*Leadership is* the ability and process to obtain desired results through influencing others to act in identified ways."	Action, Characteristic
Barge and Fairhurst 2008, 228, 232	"Leadership as a lived and experienced social activity … leadership as a co-created, performative, contextual, and attributional process where the ideas articulated in talk or action are recognized by others as progressing tasks that are important to them."	Action,

Barker 2001, 491	"Leadership ... defined as a process of transformative change where the ethics of individuals are integrated into the mores of a community as a means of evolutionary social development."	Action
Barker 2002, 90, 106, 110, 113, 118–119	"Leadership is a means for individuals to explore, to understand, to modify, and to articulate their own ethics, and compare them with the ethics of other individuals. ... Leadership ... a process of transformative change where the ethics of individuals are integrated into the mores of a community as a means of evolutionary social development ... also ... defined as a social relationship."	Action, State
Barnard 1938, 283	"Leadership ... is the indispensable social essence that gives common meaning to common purpose, that creates the incentive that makes other incentives effective, that infuses the subjective aspect of countless decisions with consistency in a changing environment, that inspires the personal conviction that produces the vital cohesiveness without which cooperation is impossible."	Characteristic
Barnard 1948, 83	"'Leadership.' ... refers to the quality of the behavior of individuals whereby they guide people or their activities in organized effort."	Action
Barnhart 1947,* 693	"**Leadership** ... the position, function, or guidance of a leader ... ability to lead."	Action, Characteristic, Role
Barrow 1977, 232	"Leadership ... defined as the behavioral process of influencing individuals or groups toward set goals, and leadership effectiveness will be defined by how well these goals are achieved."	Action

Bass 1960, 90	"When the goal of one member, A, is that of changing another member, B; or when B's change in behavior will reward A or reinforces A's behavior, A's effort to obtain the goal is leadership. … Leadership is conceived as an interaction between A and B rather than merely an act by A, because whether or not A reaches his goal involves activity by B. B's activity will reinforce A's behavior, modify A's subsequent actions. … If A's goal is to change B, A can be observed attempting to change B; this is attempted leadership. B may actually change his behavior as a consequence of A's efforts; this is successful leadership. B's change may result in B's satisfaction, reward, or goal attainment; this is effective leadership."	Action, Effect
Bass 1981, 16	"Leadership is an interaction between members of a group. … Leadership, a universal phenomenon."	Action, Phenomenon
Bass 1990, 19	"Leadership is an interaction between two or more members of a group that often involves a structuring or restructuring of the situation and the perceptions and expectations of the members."	Action

Bass, B. M. and Bass R. 2008, 7, 14, 23, 25	"Leadership is a universal phenomenon ... 'leadership' refers to a ... concept ... can include headship ... includes the many ways it is exerted by leaders and heads and the various sources of power ... heads lead as a consequence of the power of the position ... Leadership is an interaction between two or more members of a group that often involves a structuring or restructuring of the situation and of the perceptions and expectations of the members ... occurs when one group member modifies the motivation or competencies of others in the group ... can be conceived as directing the attention of other members to goals and the paths to achieve them."	Action, Concept, Effect, Phenomenon, Role
Bastardoz and Van Vugt 2019, 82	"Leadership as adaptive solutions to various kinds of organizational challenges associated with group living."	Effect
Bavelas 1960, 497	"Leadership ... consists not so much in the making of decisions ... as ... maintaining the operational effectiveness of decision-making systems."	Action
Beal, Bohlen, and Randabaugh 1962, 36	"Leadership ... is the process of influencing people by ideas."	Action
Bennis 1959, 295	"For our purposes leadership can be defined as the process by which an agent induces a subordinate to behave in a desired manner."	Action
Bennis 1961, 150	"Leadership is the fulcrum on which the demands of the individual and the demands of the organization are balanced."	Concept

Bennis 1989, 39–41	"Leadership is *a guiding vision ... passion ... integrity ... curiosity* and *daring*."	Characteristic
Bennis 2007, 3–4	"Leadership is ... a tripod—a leader or leaders, followers, and the common goal they want to achieve."	Concept
Bingham 1927, 245, 247, 258	"Leadership is the organization of the activities of a group for the achievement of a common purpose ... implies ability to define the ultimate objective and also the immediate objective ... involves both strategy and tactics ... elements ... Some are intellectual ... social-elements ... which imply ... impact of personalities ... a group of qualities."	Action, Characteristic
Birnbaum 2013, 256	"Leadership ... an interaction that influences others through noncoercive means ... a form of influence."	Action, Effect
Blackmar 1911, 626	"Leadership ... The centralization of efforts in one person as an expression of the power of all ... a powerful agent of social control. A few brains ... do the thinking for the rest who follow through imitation or lack of powers of initiative ... what A or B thinks, says, or does."	Action, Effect
Blanchard 2010, xvi	"Leadership as *the capacity to influence others by unleashing their power and potential to impact the greater good*."	Characteristic
Blondel 1987, 2–3, 13, 25	"Political leadership ... is ... a phenomenon of ... power because it consists of the ability of the one or few who are at the top to make others do a number of things (positively or negatively) that they would not or at least might not have done ... a behavioural concept ... consists of actions designed to modify the environment."	Action, Characteristic, Concept, Phenomenon, Role

Bogardus 1927, 174–175	"Leadership means vertical social distance."	Role
Bogardus 1928, 573	"Leadership is … influence of one person over other persons … types of stimuli … by which one person is instrumental in changing the attitudes of other persons. Leadership is the setting up by one person of unusual or original behavior patterns which are responded to, accepted, adapted by other persons. Leadership is the creating and setting forth of exceptional behavior patterns in such a way that numbers of persons respond to them and construct similar patterns of behavior for themselves."	Action, Effect
Bogardus 1929, 377–381	"Leadership is the special influence that one person exercises over other persons … manifested when one human being arouses the dormant attitudes of other persons, changes the attitudes of others, or arouses new attitudes in others … a social process … social stimulation which causes a number of people to set out toward an old goal with new zest or a new goal with hopeful courage … the antecedent as well as … interstimulation … interplay of attitudes."	Action, Effect

Bogardus 1934, 3–6	"Leadership is personality in action under group conditions ... includes dominant personality traits ... interaction between specific traits of one person and other traits of the many, in such a way that the course of action of the many is changed by the one. ... In fact, personality may be divided into leadership and followership ... what are leadership traits in one social situation may be followership traits in another ... In general, we may say that the more active physical and mental phases of personality comprise one's stock of leadership traits and that the less active are followership qualities. ... Leadership is a group phenomenon ... a product of group life ... also a social process ... in which the activities of the many are organized to move in a specific direction by the one ... at every stage the followers exert an influence, often a changing counter-influence, upon the leader."	Action, Characteristic, Effect, Phenomenon
Boone 1977, 110–111, 113	"Leadership ... is a special application of management ... the 'extra something' that managers must be able to do ... a unique control behavior that is directed to the management of human resources ... a special way of behaving."	Action, Characteristic
Bowers and Seashore 1966, 240	"Concept of leadership ... consists of behavior ... by one member of a group toward another member or members of the group, which advances some joint aim ... a large aggregation of separate behaviors."	Action, Concept

Braddy, Gooty, Fleenor, and Yammarino 2014, 387	"Leadership is a multi-faceted phenomenon."	Phenomenon
Bradley, Allen, Hamilton, S., and Filgo 2006, 13	"Leadership … the abilities of instilling trust, providing direction, and delegating responsibility."	Characteristic
Bratton, Grint, and Nelson, D. L. 2005, 1, 6, 13, 14, 311–313	"Leadership is an elusive concept … a process … wherein an individual persuades others to do something they would not otherwise do … a relational phenomenon … an ongoing interaction among the leader, the followers, and the context … an activity."	Action, Concept, Phenomenon
Brewer 2014, 45	"Leadership is a complex interaction between leaders and their followers … Followers are co-creators of leadership."	Action
Brown 2018, 99	"Ultimately, leadership is about bidirectional influence."	Effect
Bundel 1930, 340	"Leadership is the art of getting troops to do certain things that are essential parts of a general plan."	Characteristic
Burns, John 1972, as cited in Paige 1977, 66	"Leadership means service to others."	Action

Burns, J. M. 1978/1979, 2, 3, 19, 43, 425	"Leadership is … phenomena … a structure of action that engages persons … leaders inducing followers to act for certain goals that represent the values and the motivations—the wants and needs, the aspirations and expectations—of both leaders and followers … inseparable from followers' needs and goals … the recognition of real need, the uncovering and exploiting of contradictions among values and between values and practice, the realigning of values, the reorganization of institutions where necessary, and the governance of change … the reciprocal process of mobilizing, by persons with certain motives and values, various economic, political, and other resources, in a context of competition and conflict, in order to realize goals independently or mutually held by both leaders and followers."	Action, Characteristic, Phenomenon
Burns J. M. 2002, as cited in Wren 2007, 28	"'Leadership as an influence process, both visible and invisible, in a society inherited, constructed, and perceived as the interaction of persons in … conditions of inequality—an interaction measured by ethical and moral values and by the degrees of realization of intended, comprehensive and durable change.'"	Action

Calder 1977, 187, 195, 197, 202	"Leadership is a prime manifestation of our bias toward perceiving personal causes for behavior. It is … something we say about other people … a label which can be applied to behavior. It locates the reasons for that behavior … a first-degree construct … a set of personal qualities … a disposition … The first stage in the attribution of leadership is therefore the observation of behavior by another and effects of this behavior … exists only as a perception."	Action, Characteristic, Concept
Campbell 1992, 25	"Leadership is actions which focus resources to create desirable opportunities."	Action
Carter, L. F. 1953, 264	"Leadership in terms of leadership behaviors."	Action
Chapin 1924, 141, 145	"Phenomena of leadership."	Phenomenon
Chemers 1997, 5	"Leadership is a process of social influence through which one person is able to enlist the aid of others in reaching a goal."	Action
Chemers 2000, 27	"Leadership is … 'a process of social influence in which one person is able to enlist the aid and support of others in the accomplishment of a common task.'"	Action
Chemers 2001, 376	"Leadership is a process of social influence through which an individual enlists and mobilizes the aid of others in the attainment of a collective goal … a collective process … exists as a response to collective need … involves obtaining and utilizing the assistance of other people … a social phenomenon."	Action, Effect, Phenomenon

Chrobot-Mason 2014, 685–686	"Leadership ... the social process for generating the direction, alignment, and commitment needed by a group to accomplish collective goals ... endorsed by members of an organization where individuals mutually agree on who will be seen as having an identity as a leader."	Action
Ciulla 2002, 341–342	"Leadership is a moral and psychological relationship but it is also a social construction."	Concept, State
Clark and Clark 1994, 19–20	"Leadership is an activity or set of activities, observable to others, that occurs in a group, organization, or institution involving a leader and followers who willingly subscribe to common purposes and work together to achieve them ... one person has a special effect on the accomplishments of a group. The ... completion of concrete tasks ... the highest use of human capabilities in the pursuit of goals."	Action, Effect
Cooley 1902, 338	"Leadership ... is ... one of many aspects in which human life ... may be studied."	Characteristic
Cooley 1909, 135	"Leadership is only salient initiative."	Characteristic
Cooper and McGaugh 1963, 209, 227, 231, 232	"Leadership is an abstraction that refers to a ... social expectation ... a phenomenon ... influence effectively exerted on others ... a social process by which the behavior of one or more individuals is determined, directly or indirectly, by another individual (or his symbol), or a group of individuals (or their symbol)."	Action, Concept, Effect, Phenomenon

Copeland 1942, 77	"Leadership is the art of dealing with human nature ... of influencing a body of people, by persuasion or example, to follow a line of action."	Characteristic
Cote 2017, 28	"Leadership ... is a process that involves influencing an individual or a group in efforts toward goal achievement."	Action
Cowley 1928, 144, 152, 154	"Leadership ... is ... many traits fashioned together as a unity ... is produced by the meeting of the proper equipment with the proper situations."	Characteristic, Effect
Cowley 1931, 304	"Traits common to all leader constellations ... traits common to leaders in all situations."	Characteristic
Cribbin 1981, v, 13	"Leadership is ... an action-oriented interpersonal process ... an influence process."	Action
Cronin 1980, 372	"Leadership is generally defined as the capacity to make things happen that would otherwise not happen."	Characteristic
Dachler 1984, 102	"*Leadership* is defined as the design, change, development of, and giving directions to social *sub*systems embedded in their environment."	Action, Effect
Daft 2002, 5, 6, 8	"Leadership is an influence relationship among leaders and followers who intend real changes and outcomes that reflect their shared purposes ... a people activity ... an everyday way of acting and thinking."	Action, State
Daft 2008, 259, 784	"*Leadership* is the ability to influence people to adopt the new behaviors needed for strategy implementation ... The ability to influence people toward the attainment of organizational goals."	Characteristic

Daft 2018, 493	"**Leadership** ... is the ability to influence people toward the attainment of goals."	Characteristic
Dansereau, Graen, and Haga 1975, 46	"Leadership as an exchange relationship which develops within the vertical dyad over time during role making activities."	State
Dansereau et al. 1995, 413	"'Leadership' is defined as occurring when a superior is able to secure satisfying performance from a subordinate."	Effect
Dasborough and Ashkanasy 2002, 629	"Leadership is ... an emotional process, where leaders display emotion and attempt to evoke emotion in their members ... Leadership is a process of social interaction where leaders attempt to influence the behavior of their followers ... leadership is ... defined in terms of basic psychology theories such as the attribution theory."	Action
Davenport 1993, as cited in McFarland, Senn, and Childress 1993, 208	"Leadership is character."	Characteristic
Davies 1982,* 719	"**Leadership** ... The position or office of a leader ... The capacity or ability to lead."	Characteristic, Role
Davis 1962, 118	"Leadership is the human factor which binds a group together and motivates it toward goals ... leadership is ... the result of complex interaction of the leader and his followers in a dynamic environment."	Characteristic, Effect

Davis and Newstrom 1985, 158	"Leadership is the process of encouraging and helping others to work enthusiastically toward objectives ... the human factor that binds a group together and motivates it toward goals ... Leadership is the ultimate act that brings to success all the potential that is in an organization and its people ... the behaviors, roles, and skills that combine to form different leadership styles ... Leadership is an important part of management."	Action, Characteristic, Role
Day 2000, 605	"Leadership is a complex interaction between individuals and their social and organizational environments."	Action
Day 2004, 840	"Leadership as a process (not a position) that involves leaders, followers, and situations."	Action
Day 2014a, 3	"Important but somewhat mysterious and elusive construct."	Concept
Day 2014b, 863	"Leadership is a process and not a person or a position."	Action
Day and Antonakis 2012, 5	"Leadership can be defined ... (a) an influencing process—and its resultant outcomes—that occurs between a leader and followers and (b) how this influencing process is explained by the leader's dispositional characteristics and behaviors, follower perceptions and attributions of the leader, and the context in which the influencing process occurs. ... the leader as person (dispositional characteristics), leader behavior, the effects of a leader, the interaction process between a leader and follower(s), and the importance of context."	Action, Characteristic, Concept, Effect

Day, Fleenor, Atwater, Sturm, and McKee 2014, 78–79	"Leadership is ... a process ... a complex interaction between people and their social and political environments."	Action, Characteristic
de Haan 2016, 508	"Leadership as *a process that is devoted to enhancing an organization's effectiveness.*"	Action
Dede and Aryanci 2014, 245	"Leadership is a social process."	Action
Department of the Army United States of America 2019, 1–13	**"Leadership is the activity of influencing people by providing purpose, direction, and motivation to accomplish the mission and improve the organization."**	Action
DeRue and Myers 2014, 834	"Leadership is a social and mutual influence process where multiple actors engage in leading-following interactions in service of accomplishing a collective goal."	Action
Dessler 2001, 291, 553	"Leadership is ... influencing others to work willingly toward achieving objectives ... one person influencing another to willingly work toward a predetermined objective."	Effect
DeVille 1984, 156	"Leadership ... the ability to capture the imagination of people, to grip the loyalty of work teams, and to inspire individuals to do more than they deemed possible before meeting the leader."	Characteristic
Dinh, Lord, Gardner, W. L., Meuser, Liden, and Hu 2014, 37	"Leadership is a ... phenomenon ... that involves multiple mediating and moderating factors ... and takes place over substantial periods of time."	Characteristic, Phenomenon

Downton 1973, 4–7, 14	"Constructs like leadership ... leadership is derived from its general contributions as a structure within the social process ... persistent patterns of social interaction, commonly called 'social systems' ... leadership ... defined as the coordinating structure of social systems."	Action, Concept
Drath and Palus 1994, 4, 6	"Leadership as a tool that people use in their relations with one another ... to make sense, to make meaning ... The process of making meaning in certain kinds of social settings constitutes leadership ... leadership as meaning-making in a community of practice."	Action
Drucker 1954, 159–160	"Leadership is the lifting of a man's vision to higher sights, the raising of a man's performance to a higher standard, the building of a man's personality beyond its normal limitations."	Effect
Drucker 1967, 168–169	"Character: foresight, self-reliance, courage ... in other words ... leadership—... of brilliance and genius ... of dedication, determination, and serious purpose."	Characteristic
Drucker 1988, abstract	"Leadership ... is performance ... Leadership is a means ... work ... thinking through the organization's mission, defining it and establishing it ... a responsibility ... the final requirement ... is to earn trust."	Action, Characteristic
DuBrin 2001, 3, 22	"Leadership is the ability to inspire confidence and support among the people who are needed to achieve organizational goals."	Characteristic

Dupuy and Dupuy 1959, 345	"Characteristics ... competence, an understanding of the human tools of the commander, insistence on high standards of training and discipline, ability to inspire their men, unquestioned personal courage, and consistent perseverance and determination in the face of adversity."	Characteristic
Eacott 2013, 91–92, 96–97	"Leadership is an epistemic label applied post-event ... an epistemic ... concept ... leadership is a means through which to bring about a better future, achieved through the manipulation, read control, of the forthcoming."	Action, Concept
Eagly and Carli 2007, 8–9	"*Leadership* entails being in charge of other people in multiple ways ... consists of influencing, motivating, organizing, and coordinating the work of others. In groups, organizations, and nations ... bringing people together to enable them to work toward shared goals."	Action, Effect, Role
Eisenhower 1968, as cited in Larson 1968, 15	"'Leadership is the ability to decide what is to be done, and then to get others to want to do it.'"	Characteristic, Effect
Emery and Brewster 1927,* 933	"**Leadership ...** The position, function, or guidance of a leader; also, ability to lead."	Action, Characteristic, Role
Epitropaki, Martin, and Thomas 2018, 111	"Leadership is ... a relational concept."	Concept
Etzioni 1965, 690	"Leadership is the ability, based on the personal qualities of the leader, to elicit the followers' voluntary compliance in a broad range of matters."	Characteristic

Fairhurst and Grant 2010, 172	"Leadership is co-constructed, a product of sociohistorical and collective meaning making."	Effect
Fiedler 1965, 115	"Leadership is a personal relationship in which one person directs, coordinates, and supervises others in the performance of a common task."	State
Fiedler 1967, 11	"Leadership is, by definition, an interpersonal relation in which power and influence are unevenly distributed so that one person is able to direct and control the actions and behaviors of others to a greater extent than they direct and control his."	State
Fischer, Dietz, and Antonakis 2017, 1727	"Leadership is a social and goal-oriented influence process, unfolding in a temporal and spatial milieu."	Action
Fitzsimmons and Callan 2020, 11	"Leadership is a relational process which extends beyond leader/follower dyads, and beyond individual organizations."	Action
Fleishman 1973, 3–4	"Definition of leadership … is: attempts at 'interpersonal influence, directed through the communication process, toward the attainment of some goal or goals.' … attempts to affect the behaviors of others … unsuccessful attempts can be operationally defined as ineffective leadership."	Action
Fleishman, Mumford, Zaccaro, Levin, Korotkin, and Hein 1991, 259, 276	"Defined leadership in terms of social problem-solving directed toward organizational goal attainment."	Action

Fleishman and Peters 1962, 127	"Any modern definition of leadership is the notion of interpersonal influence. Leadership acts occur when one individual, whether or not he is in a formally designated 'leadership position,' attempts to influence the behavior of others toward some goal."	Action, Effect
Flexner 1987,* 1093	"**Leadership** ... the position or function of a leader ... ability to lead ... an act or instance of leading; guidance; direction ... the leaders of a group."	Action, Characteristic, Role
Follett 1933/1949, 50–52, 55, 57, 59	"Requisites of leadership ... knowledge of your job ... ability to grasp a total situation ... ability to organize all the forces ... and make them serve a common purpose ... personal qualities ... ability to share ... conviction with others, ability to make purpose articulate ... personal qualities ... tenacity, sincerity, fair dealings with all, steadfastness of purpose, depth of conviction, control of temper, tact, steadiness in stormy periods, ability to meet emergencies, power to draw forth and develop the latent possibilities of others ... three kinds of leadership: ... of position, of personality and ... of function. ... how and when to praise, how and when to point out mistakes, what attitude to take toward failures."	Action, Characteristic, Effect, Role
Friedrich 1961, 6, 20–21	"Political leadership, is a function of the political order ... three ... roles of leadership ... initiating, maintaining and protecting ... to which correspond ... behaviors of the followership: imitating, obeying and acclaiming."	Action, Role

Friend and Guralnik 1951,* 829	"**Leadership** ... the position or guidance of a leader ... the ability to lead."	Action, Characteristic, Role
Funk 1893,* 1011	"**Leadership** ... The office or a position of a leader; ability to lead; guidance."	Action, Characteristic, Role
Galinsky, Jordan, and Sivanathan 2008, 284	"Define it as influencing, motivating, and enabling a group of individuals to contribute to the success of a common goal or shared purpose ... a social phenomenon ... requires the presence of others ... to influence, motivate, and mobilize."	Action, Effect, Phenomenon, Role
Gardner, J. W. 1986, 6	"Leadership ... is the process of persuasion and example by which an individual (or leadership team) induces a group to take action that is in accord with the leader's purposes or the shared purposes of all."	Action
Gardner, J. W. 1988, 4	"Leadership is the process of persuasion or example by which an individual (or leadership team) induces a group to pursue objectives held by the leader or shared by the leader and his or her followers."	Action
Gardner, W. L., Lowe, Moss, Mahoney, and Cogliser 2010, 951	"Leadership is a ... socially constructed process."	Action
Garretsen, Stoker, and Weber 2020, 1, 9	"Leadership is a means to an end."	Action

Gibb 1947, 267–268, 284	"'Leadership' is a concept applied to the personality-environment relation to describe the situation when one, or at most a very few, personalities are so placed in the environment that his, or their, 'will, feeling, and insight direct and control others in the pursuit of a cause' ... a function of the social situation and a function of personality ... in interaction; no additive concept is adequate to explain the phenomenon ... A leader is a member of a group on whom the group confers a certain status, and leadership describes the role by which the duties of this status are fulfilled."	Action, Concept, Effect, Phenomenon, Role, State
Gibb 1954, 910, 914	"Leadership is a means ... Leadership is an interactional phenomenon arising when group formation takes place ... Leadership is a function of personality, and of the social situation, and of these two in interaction."	Action, Effect, Phenomenon

Gibb 1958, 102–104, 109	"Leadership ... as a group function. Leadership emerges ... as part of a more diffuse differentiation of roles by which group members ... achieve group goals and satisfy their individual group-invested needs. Leadership is part of the problem-solving machinery of groups ... a concept applied to the structure of a group to describe the situation when some personalities are so placed in the group that their will, feeling, and insight are perceived to direct and control others in the pursuit of common ends ... is ... applied to the interaction of two or more persons ... a function of personality ... also a function of the social system ... a function of these two in interaction ... Leadership means ... leaders are perceived to contribute positively to the satisfaction of individual's group-invested needs ... role differentiation ... is part and parcel of a group's locomotion toward its goals and thus toward the satisfaction of needs of individual members ... a concept applied to the interaction of two more persons, when ... he, or they, come to control and direct the actions of the others in the pursuit of common ends."	Action, Concept, Effect, Role

Gibb 1969, 261, 268, 270–271	"Leadership is a means … the particular attributes of personality, ability, and skill which differentiate him perceptually from other members of the group … one facet … of this larger process of role differentiation … concept applied to the … interaction influencing the actions of others in a shared approach to common or compatible goals … role behavior … a function of personal attributes and social system in dynamic interaction … that aspect of role differentiation by which all or a large number of group members make use of individual contributions which they perceive to have value in moving the group toward its goals … Leadership exists … whenever its norms and structure allow the special abilities and resources of one or a few members to be used in the interests of many or all … applies only when … voluntarily accepted or when it is in a 'shared direction' … Leadership is an interactional phenomenon … leadership is a function of personality and of the social situation, and of these two in interaction."	Action, Characteristic, Concept, Effect, Phenomenon, Role
Gini 1997, 321, 324	"Leadership is a delicate combination of the process, the techniques of leadership, the person, and the specific talents and traits of a/the leader, and the general requirements of the job itself … concept … phenomenon."	Action, Characteristic, Phenomenon, Role
Goffee and Jones, G. 2001, 148	"Leadership … is: part of a duality or a relationship."	State

Gove 1961,* 1283	"**Leadership** ... the office or position of a leader ... the quality of a leader: capacity to lead ... the act or an instance of leading ... a group of persons who lead."	Action, Characteristic, Role
Graen 2010, as cited in Graen, Rowold, and Heinitz 2010, 563	"Leadership is ... informal emergent influence that can be activated by problem situations demanding leader-member cooperative, extra role action much beyond the ordinary action feasible from formal supervisor and subordinate or coworker problem situations, e. g., 'when the beehive hits the fan.'"	Action, Effect
Graen and Uhl-Bien 1991, 28	"**Leadership** ... an 'influential increment' over and above that which is formally prescribed in the work unit ... extra influence ... from extremely effective, where the leadership influence dominates the structural influences to non-existent, where no additional increment of influence is exerted."	Effect

Greenleaf 1972, 10, 16, 27, 30	"Leadership: building purpose and challenging with opportunity, judicious use of incentives, astute ordering of priorities and allocating resources where they count the most ... provides the encouragement and the shelter for venturing and risking the unpopular ... gives support for ethical behavior and creative ways for doing things better ... Leadership: Conceptual and Operational ... managing and administering ... Leadership ... going out ahead to show the way, is more conceptual than operating ... leadership ... will ... seek out, encourage, discriminately judge, and reward when successful all genuine initiatives ... and penalize, to the point of drying up or radically reorganizing ... dynamics of leadership ... vision ... values ... staying power."	Action, Characteristic, Concept
Greenleaf 1977, 109, 256	"*Leadership*—going out ahead to show the way ... one individual has a better than average sense of what should be done now and is willing to take the risk to say, 'Let us do *this now.*'"	Action, Characteristic

Grint 2000, 6, 13, 27	"Leadership is an essentially social phenomenon ... an invention ... Leadership is ... a product of the imagination ... leadership might better be considered as an art ... four ... features ... : the invention of an identity, the formulation of a strategic vision, the construction of organizational tactics, and the deployment of persuasive mechanisms to ensure followers actually follow."	Action, Characteristic, Concept, Effect, Phenomenon
Grint 2005, 5	"Leadership is 'an essentially contested concept.'"	Concept
Grint 2010a, 13, 85, 105, 135, 137	"Leadership is ... a relational phenomenon: without followers, you cannot be a leader ... leadership is a relationship ... the property and consequence of a community ... the art of engaging a group or community into facing its wicked problems."	Characteristic, Effect, Phenomenon, State
Grint 2010b, 306–308, 313	"'Leadership (... persuading the collective to take responsibility for collective problems) ... the ability to solve problems, act decisively and to know what to do ... the art of engaging a community in facing up to complex collective problems ... engaging the collective in facing up to its collective problems."	Action, Characteristic, Effect
Gronn 1996, 9	"Leadership is a form of direct or indirect influence ... a significant effect on an individual or group's well-being, interests, policies or behaviour."	Effect
Gronn 1997, 276	"Leadership is an emergent, attributed status ... influence deemed legitimate by followers."	Effect, Role

Gronn 2002, 428	"Leadership is ... a status ascribed to one individual, an aggregate of separate individuals, sets of small numbers of individuals acting in concert or larger plural-member organizational units."	Role
Guralnik 1970,* 801	"**Leadership** ... the position or guidance of a leader ... the ability to lead ... the leaders of a group."	Action, Characteristic, Role
Hackman and Johnson 2013, 11	"Leadership is human (symbolic) communication that modifies the attitudes and behaviors of others in order to meet shared group goals and needs."	Action, Effect
Haimann and Hilgert 1977, 11–12	"Leadership is the ability one possesses to influence the opinions, attitudes, and behavior of others. ... more a process than a positional relationship ... includes what the followers or group members think and do."	Action, Characteristic, Concept, State
Halpin 2011, 479	"Leadership involves one person influencing another to engage in some purposeful or goal-directed behavior."	Effect
Hamstra, Van Yperen, Wisse, and Sassenberg 2014, 415	"Leadership is generally acknowledged to involve influencing followers' motivation and moving followers toward (collective) goal attainment."	Effect
Harvey 2011, 199	"Leadership ... an interaction between leaders and followers—is the most complex of human relationships."	Action, State
Heifetz 1988, 37	"Leadership as an activity ... the mobilization of the resources of a people or of an organization to make progress on the difficult problems it faces."	Action

Heifetz 1994, 14, 20, 22	"Leadership is a ... concept ... an activity—the activity of a citizen from any walk of life mobilizing people to do something ... requires orchestrating ... conflicts among and within the interested parties."	Action, Concept
Heifetz 2007, 34	"Leadership as the activity of mobilizing progress ... the work of mobilizing people's adaptive capacity to tackle tough problems and thrive."	Action
Heifetz and Sinder 1988, 195	"Leadership ... not simply the fulfilling of one's authority ... calls for mobilizing the group's resources to face, define, and resolve its problems."	Action, Role
Helmick 1924, 149	"Leadership is the art of leading."	Characteristic
Hemphill 1949a, 5	"Leadership ... the behavior of an individual while he is involved in directing group activities."	Action
Hemphill 1949b, 225	"Successful leadership ... is the interaction of the leader who possesses a given set of personal attributes and the group whose efficient functioning demands that particular combination of attributes which results in successful leadership."	Action
Hemphill 1961, 201–202	"Leadership is a ... mixture of social behaviors ... A successful leadership act is an attempted leadership act which has been followed ... An effective leadership act has ... initiated structure into interaction ... also contributed to the group's solution of a mutual problem."	Action
Hemphill and Coons 1957, 7	"Leadership ... is the behavior of an individual when he is directing the activities of a group toward a shared goal."	Action

Hersey and Blanchard 1972, 68	"Leadership is the process of influencing the activities of an individual or a group in efforts toward goal achievement in a given situation."	Action
Hersey and Blanchard 1974, 22	"Leadership is a 'process of influencing the activities of an individual or a group in efforts toward goal achievement in a given situation' … in any situation where someone is trying to influence the behavior of another individual or group, leadership is occurring. Thus, everyone attempts leadership."	Action
Hersey and Blanchard 1988, 86, 128	"Leadership is the process of influencing the activities of an individual or a group in efforts toward goal achievement in a given situation … an attempt to influence, for whatever reason."	Action
Hersey and Blanchard 2001, 9, 79, 126	"Leadership occurs whenever one person attempts to influence the behavior of an individual or group, regardless of the reason … the process of influencing the activities of an individual or a group in efforts toward goal achievement in a given situation … an attempt to influence people, individually and in groups, for whatever reason."	Action
Hersey, Blanchard, and Johnson 2008, 62	"Leadership is the process of influencing the activities of an individual or a group toward reaching goal achievement in a given situation."	Action
Hersey, Blanchard, and Natemeyer 1979, 418	"Leadership is … the process of influencing the activities of an individual or a group in efforts toward goal achievement."	Action

Hesselbein 2002, 3, 21, 35, 69, 95	*"Leadership is a matter of how to be* ... leadership is all about valuing relationships, ... valuing people ... a responsibility shared by all members of an organization."	Action, Characteristic, Role
Hitler 1925, as cited in Murphy, J. 1939, 102	"The art of leadership, as displayed by really great popular leaders in all ages, consists in consolidating the attention of the people against a single adversary and taking care that nothing will split up that attention into sections. The more the militant energies of the people are directed towards one objective the more will new recruits join the movement, attracted by the magnetism of its unified action, and thus the striking power will be all the more enhanced ... The leader of genius must have the ability to make different opponents appear as if they belonged to one category."	Characteristic
Hogan, R., Curphy, and Hogan, J. 1994, 1	"Leadership involves persuading other people to set aside for a period of time their individual concerns and to pursue a common goal that is important for the responsibilities and welfare of a group ... morally neutral ... persuasion ... only occurs when others willingly adopt, for a period of time, the goals of a group as their own ... concerns building cohesive and goal-oriented teams."	Action, Effect
Hogan, R. and Kaiser 2005, 169–170 172	"Leadership is a ... phenomenon ... an adaptive tool for individual and group survival ... the ability to build and maintain a group that performs well relative to its competition ... group performance ... is the most appropriate way to define and evaluate leadership."	Action, Characteristic, Effect, Phenomenon

Hogg 2001, 185, 189, 194	"Leadership is ... a product of individual information processing ... leadership is a relational property within groups (i.e., leaders exist because of followers and followers exist because of leaders) ... some individuals or cliques have disproportionate power and influence to set agenda, define identity, and mobilize people to achieve collective goals ... a group process ... influencing other people ... a process of influence that enlists and mobilizes the involvement of others in the attainment of collective goals."	Action, Characteristic, Effect
Hogg 2008, 63	"Leadership is a ... social psychological process where an individual has disproportionate influence over a group."	Action
Hogg 2013, 241–244, 257	"Leadership is ... a group process of social influence ... a ... phenomenon, ... people interacting with and influencing others in the context of a group ... requires there to be one or more individuals who influence the behavior of other individuals or the group as a whole ... development and communication of an idea (vision, norm, etc.) that is positively received, freely accepted, internalized, and adhered to by the group ... an individual (or set of individuals) forging and communicating a vision for the group that other members internalize as a part of who they are and how they should behave."	Action, Effect, Phenomenon

Hogg, Martin, and Weeden 2003, 19–20	"Leadership is ... a group process ... a relationship in which some people are able to influence others to embrace, as their own, new values, attitudes and goals, and to exert effort on behalf of, and in pursuit of, those values, attitudes and goals ... an essential feature of social groups."	Action, Characteristic, State
Hollander 1964, 1, 3	"Leadership is a relationship between a person exerting influence and those who are influenced ... within the framework of group process ... Leadership is a phenomenon."	Action, Phenomenon, State
Hollander 1978, 1–4	"Leadership is a process of influence between a leader and those who are followers ... behaviors ... must include the reactions of followers ... authority over others in the case of organizations and nations, and as dominance among less organized groups as animals and children ... concept ... involves someone who exerts influence, and those who are influenced."	Action, Concept, Effect, Role
Hollander 1986, 39–40, 49	"Leadership involves ... the leader's actions ... also ... a system of relationships including followers, their expectation and commitments, and task demands ... a social process."	Action, State
Hollander and Julian 1968, 890	"Leadership ... implies ... a ... influence relationship between two or more persons ... conceived as ... one representation of the more general phenomenon of interpersonal influence."	Concept, State

Hollander and Julian 1969, 388, 390, 395	"Leadership ... an influence relationship between two, or usually more, persons who depend upon on one another for the attainment of certain mutual goals within a group situation ... an influence process, involving an explicit exchange relationship over time."	Action, State
Hollander and Offermann 1990, 179–180	"Leadership ... a process involving the direction and maintenance of collective activity ... a system of relationships with constraints as well as opportunities."	Action, Characteristic, State
House 1995, 413	"General leadership is behavior of individuals that gives purpose, meaning, and guidance to collectivities by articulating a collective vision that appeals to ideological values, motives, and self-perceptions of followers resulting in (1) the infusion of values into organizations and work, (2) unusual levels of effort on the part of followers above and beyond their normal role or position requirements, and (3) follower willingness to forego self-interest and make significant personal sacrifices in the interest of a collective vision."	Action, Effect
House, Javidan, Hanges, and Dorfman 2002, 5	"Organizational leadership ... 'the ability of an individual to influence, motivate, and enable others to contribute toward the effectiveness and success of the organizations of which they are members ... the phenomenon of organizational leadership."	Characteristic, Phenomenon

Hughbank and Horn 2013, 245–247	"Leadership is an art ... a natural phenomenon and a learned attribute ... a global concept ... the action of convincing others to do something in a certain context that leads to a positive and successful organizational outcome."	Action, Characteristic, Concept, Phenomenon
Hughes, Ginnett, and Curphy 1993, 1, 6, 8, 52–54, 89	"Leadership is a process ... something happening as a result of the interaction between a leader and followers ... a process involving various aspects of power and influence tactics ... a ... phenomenon involving the leader, the followers, and the situation ... a social influence process shared among all members of a group ... **LEADERSHIP IS A SCIENCE AND AN ART** ... includes actions and influences ... the process of influencing others toward the achievement of group goals."	Action, Characteristic, Effect, Phenomenon, Role
Hughes, Ginnett, and Curphy 2009, 6	"Leadership as 'the process of influencing an organized group toward accomplishing its goals.'"	Action
Hunt, J. B. 2000, 94–95	"Leadership is ... a reciprocally negotiated relationship between leader and follower that is contingent, situational, transactional and, at times, transformational for both leader and follower depending on the common goals."	State
Ikenberry 1996, 388, 396	"Leadership ... has two ... elements— power and purpose ... ability to shape, directly or indirectly, the interests or actions or others ... a second element ... marshalling of power capabilities and material resources ... the use of power to orchestrate the actions of a group toward a collective end."	Action, Characteristic

Jacobs 1970, 232, 338–340	"Leadership is ... an interaction between persons in which one presents information ... that the other becomes convinced that his outcomes (benefits/costs ratio) will be improved if he behaves in the manner suggested or desired ... an interactional phenomenon ... concept ... persuasive communication ...—not necessarily verbal—which convinces the influence recipient that he will benefit in some way if he behaves as the influence initiator wishes ... a transaction between the leader and the group."	Action, Concept, Effect, Phenomenon
Jacobs and Jaques 1990, 281–282	"Leadership is a process of giving purpose [meaningful direction] to collective effort, and causing willing effort to be expended to achieve purpose ... an influence process which is a type of role behavior. ... a systems requirement ... related to the process of organizing and gaining collective unity of movement ... an exchange of information about what ought to be done (or how it ought to be done, or some other discretionary issue) that, if successful, impacts on the belief systems which support action."	Action, Effect, Role

Jago 1982, 315–316	"Leadership is … a process and a property … *process* … the use of noncoercive influence to direct and coordinate the activities of the members of an organized group toward the accomplishment of group objectives … *property* … the set of qualities or characteristics attributed to those who are perceived to successfully employ such influence."	Action, Characteristic, Effect
Janda 1960, 345, 348, 358	"A conception of leadership as a particular type of power relationship … type of group phenomenon … concerned with the activities of 'salient' group members—those who could be positively differentiated from other group members on the basis of behavior, perceptions, group structure, or personal factors … a group member's perception that another group member has the right to prescribe behavior patterns for the former regarding his activity as a member of a particular group."	Action, Concept, Phenomenon, State
Jennings 1944, 433	"Leadership … a manner of interacting with others, a social process of interaction involving behavior *by* and *toward* the individual 'lifted' to a leader role by other individuals."	Action
Jennings 1947, 32, 43	"Leadership phenomena 'happen;' … behaviors … a process … between the individual and *specific* other persons, resulting in interaction between them."	Action, Phenomenon
Jewell and Abate 2001,* 968	"**Leadership** … the action of leading a group of people or an organization … the state or position of being a leader … the leaders of an organization, country, etc. … the ability to lead skillfully."	Action, Characteristic, Role, State

Jones, G. R. and George 2007, 357	"Leadership is the process by which an individual exerts influence over other people and inspires, motivates, and directs their activities to help achieve group or organizational goals."	Action
Kan and Parry 2004, 468, 486	"Characteristics of the leadership phenomenon ... a dynamic process occurring in dynamic contexts."	Action, Characteristic, Phenomenon
Katz and Kahn 1966, 301–302, 308–309, 334	"Leadership is a relational concept ... Without followers there can be no leader ... *the essence of organizational leadership to be the influential* increment over and above mechanical compliance *with the routine directives of the organization* ... is always a combined function of social structural factors and of the particular characteristics of the individuals ... When people are influenced to engage in organizationally relevant behavior, leadership has occurred ... Leadership ... as any *act of influence on a matter of organizational relevance* ... includes many routine acts of supervision; ... *influential increment* which goes beyond routine and taps bases of power beyond those that are organizationally decreed ... include *referent power,* ... personal liking between leader and follower, and *expert power,* ... knowledge and ability of the leader."	Action, Characteristic, Concept, Effect, Role
Kelemen, Matthews, and Breevaart 2020, 1–2	"Leadership is a daily and fluctuating phenomenon ... a ... process."	Action, Phenomenon
Kellerman and Webster, S. W. 2001, 487	"Leadership as a process ... in which the leader(s) and followers interact ... to generate change."	Action, Effect

Kilburg and Donohue 2011, 15	*"Leadership is a complex, multidimensional, emergent process in which the leader(s), follower(s), and other formal and informal stakeholders in a human enterprise use their characteristics, capabilities, thoughts, feelings, and behaviors to create mutually influencing relationships that enable them to coevolve strategies, tactics, structures, processes, directions, and other methods of building and managing human enterprises with the goal of producing adaptive success in their chosen niche(s) in the competitive, evaluative, and evolving global ecology of organizations."*	Action
Kim and Mauborgne 1992, 123	"Qualities of leadership ... ability to hear what is left unspoken, humility, commitment, ... looking at reality from many vantage points, the ability to create an organization that draws out the unique strengths of every member."	Characteristic, Concept
King 1990, 43, 50	"Leadership is ... phenomena ... a complex interactive process with behavioural, relational, and Situational elements."	Action, Phenomenon
Kirkpatrick and Locke 1991, 58–59	"Leadership is a ... demanding activity ... a demanding, unrelenting job."	Action, Role
Kochan, Schmidt, and DeCotiis 1975, 285	"Leadership is an influence process whereby O's actions change P's behavior and P views the influence attempt as being legitimate and the change as being consistent with P's goals."	Action, Effect

Kodish 2006, 464	"Leadership is ... the ability to act purposively and ethically as the situation requires ... is about understanding the world in a richer and broader sense ... a ... combination of traits, behaviors, principles, and relationships."	Action, Characteristic, Concept, State
Komives, Lucas, and McMahon, 1998, 20–21	"Leadership as *a process of people together attempting to accomplish change or make a difference to benefit the common good.*"	Action
Komives, Lucas, and McMahon 2013, vii	"Leadership is a relational and ethical process of people together attempting to accomplish positive change ... is about relationships."	Action, State
Kort 2008, 422–423	"Leadership is a social relation ... A leader ... makes good decisions and suggestions ... that are endorsed by others ... This relation, then, occurs by way of an event—the plural action."	State
Kotter 1988, 5	"Leadership ... as the process of moving a group (or groups) of people in some direction through (mostly) noncoercive means."	Action
Kouzes and Posner 1990, 24, 26	"Leadership is a reciprocal process in that it occurs between people ... about leaders ... about followers ... a ... bond between leaders and constituents."	Action, Role, State
Kouzes and Posner 2003a, 3	"Leadership is a reciprocal process ... occurs between people."	Action
Kouzes and Posner 2003b, xxviii, 20	"Leadership is ... a process ... LEADERSHIP IS A RELATIONSHIP Leadership is an identifiable set of skills and practices ... Leadership is a relationship between those who aspire to lead and those who choose to follow."	Action, Characteristic, State

Kouzes and Posner 2016, 49	"Leadership is ... an observable pattern of actions and behaviors ... a definable set of skills and abilities."	Action, Characteristic,
Krech and Crutchfield 1948, 436	"Leadership is a *relationship* between subparts of the whole structure ... of the group situation ... and ... the needs and perceptions of the individual members ... also *the psychology of the leader.*"	State
Lapierre and Carsten 2014, ix	"Leadership is a process of mutual influence ... where leaders and followers work together to advance common objectives."	Action
Lee and Fahr 2019, 417	"Leadership is a network-property."	Characteristic
Levi 2001, 174	"Leadership is a process in which an individual influences the progress of other group members toward the attainment of a goal."	Action
Levi 2011, 166	"Leadership is a process in which an individual influences the progress of group members toward attainment of a goal ... or set of functions that may be performed by many of a team's members."	Action, Role
Lobo 2014, 363	"Leadership ... the wielding of political power to influence, direct, or alter the authoritative values within that society."	Action
Loeb 1993, as cited in McFarland, Senn, and Childress 1993, 212	"Leadership means setting goals for an organization, finding people who can fulfill those goals, and inspiring them to meet those goals."	Action, Effect
Lombardi 1969, as cited in Hornung and Reed 2006, 148	"Leadership is defined as the ability to direct people, but more important to have that direction accepted."	Characteristic, Effect

Long 1963, 4	"Leadership is … the transformation of doubts into psychological grounds of cooperative common action."	Effect
Lord, Brown and Harvey 2001, 283	"Leadership as a *'social perception, grounded in social-cognitive psychological theory that produces an influence increment for the perceived leader.'*"	Concept
Lord and Maher 1991, 4, 11	"Leadership as resulting from a social-perceptual process … *of being perceived by others as a leader* … an outcome of the social-cognitive processes … involves behaviors, traits, characteristics, and outcomes produced by leaders as these elements are interpreted by followers."	Action, Concept, Effect
Lussier and Achua 2007, 6	"Leadership is the influencing process of leaders and followers to achieve organizational objectives through change."	Action
Lussier and Achua 2010, 6, 489	"Leadership is the influencing process *between* leaders and followers … a two-way street."	Action
Mackenzie 2010, 1050	"Leadership is a … set of definable processes … an individual and an organizational phenomenon."	Action, Phenomenon
Mann 1927, as cited in Moore 1927, 127	"Leadership is the peculiar genius of an individual finding its greatest effectiveness in leading others."	Characteristic

Manning and Curtis 2015, 1, 2, 11, 558	"Leadership is a concept … social influence … It is initiating and guiding … **establishing a direction** (planning), **aligning people and resources** (organizing), and **energizing people to accomplish results** (directing) … social influence; showing the way or course of action; causing to follow by ideas and deeds; influencing through instruction, heroic feats, and force of will, magnified by the component of caring about the task to be done and the welfare of others; the functions or processes."	Action, Concept, Effect, Role
Marieta, Bagus, and Riantoputra 2019, 108	"Leadership is a relationship process whereby leaders influence the followers to achieve common goals."	Action
Marion and Uhl-Bien 2001, 406	"Leadership … defined … as tending to growth, fitness, innovation, and the future of organizations."	Action

Markus, Allison, and Eylon 2004, 1462–1463	"Leadership ... a special case of social influence involving ... interaction between the leader, the followers, and the group to which they belong ... leaders and followers influence one another and exchange resources with the purpose of attaining collective and personal goals ... a positive social process in which all people in the group, whether leaders or followers, benefit from the outcomes of their interactions."	Action, Effect
Marturano, Wren, and Harvey 2013, 1	"Leadership as an asymmetrical (albeit interactive and mutual) influence process that serves to articulate, clarify, and facilitate the accomplishment of a group's (organization's, community's, society's) objectives (including, importantly, survival)."	Action
Maxwell 1998, 17	"Leadership is influence—nothing more, nothing less."	Effect
Maxwell 2013, 2, 4, 51, 67, 146, 171	"Leadership is influence ... a process ... action ... encouragement ... what a person does with and for others ... an exciting journey."	Action, Effect
McCauley 2010, 7	"Leadership is a broad and evolving concept ... leadership can be understood as a social process for generating the direction, alignment, and commitment needed for individuals to work together productively toward collective outcomes."	Action, Concept
McCauley and Fick-Cooper 2015, 2	"Leadership ... is a *social process* that enables individuals to work together as a cohesive group to produce collective results—results they could never achieve working as individuals."	Action

McCrimmon 2011, para. 1, 4	"Leadership, an act or series of acts that moves people in a certain direction ... **discrete acts of influence** ... providing direction."	Action
Medina 2011, 80	"Leadership ... as an art form, where the important insight comes in appreciating that the same situation will never occur twice."	Characteristic
Meindl 1990, 162–164, 166	"Leadership is viewed as an explanatory category to which attributions are made to account for a variety of organizational events and occurrences ... a concept that can be invoked to understand how a certain state of affairs or set of outcomes was produced ... a ... concept ... people use to understand organizations."	Concept
Meindl 1993, 97–99	"Leadership ... as an experience undergone by followers ... an overlay that followers place onto an otherwise formally defined hierarchical relationship with the supervisor ... an enrichment ... of the relationship ... the emergence among followers of a state of mind, an experience they undergo ... emerges in the minds of followers. Without the experience, without being in a state of leadership, followership does not exist, and hence leadership cannot be said to have emerged ... the emergence of an ideology."	Action, Concept, State

Meindl 1995, 330–332	"Leadership as a social construction … part of the way actors experience organizational processes … in the eyes of the beholder: followers, not the leader—and not researchers—define it … an emergent phenomenon … emerged when followers construct their experiences in … leadership concepts—… when they interpret their relationship as having a leadership-followership dimension."	Action, Concept, Phenomenon
Meindl, Ehrlich, and Dukerich 1985, 78, 79	"Leadership is … an explanatory concept used to understand organizations as causal systems … a permanently entrenched part of the socially constructed reality that we bring to bear in our analysis of organizations … a perception that people attempt to make sense out of organizationally relevant phenomena … an explanatory category that can be used to explain and account for organizational activities and outcomes."	Concept
Meindl, Pastor, and Mayo 2004, 1348	"The interpretations, reactions, and attributions of followers and observers … define leadership … the mental representations that followers (not leaders) carry in their heads about the centrality of leadership to organizational activities, … implicit theories about what good leadership is, and … views about the characteristics of specific leaders."	Action, Concept
Michaelis 1963,* 769	"**Leadership** … The office, position, or capacity of a leader; authoritative control; guidance … Ability to lead, exert authority, etc. … A group of leaders."	Action, Characteristic, Effect, Role

Middlebrooks, Allen, McNutt, and Morrison 2020, 2	"**Leadership** is the process of influencing others toward a common vision."	Action
Miller and Sardais 2011, 176	"Conception of leadership ... *Leadership occurs when someone imparts his or her convictions to another.*"	Action, Concept
Mish 1983,* 679	"**Leadership** ... the office or position of a leader ... the capacity to lead ... LEADERS."	Characteristic, Role
Mish 1993/1994,* 661	"**Leadership** ... the office or position of a leader ... the capacity to lead ... the act or an instance of leading ... LEADERS."	Action, Characteristic, Role
Mitroff 1978, 131, 134,	"Leadership is an ill-structured concept ... the management of large-scale, ill-structured problems, has no absolute starting or ending point."	Action, Concept
Moltchanova 2015, 47	"Leadership as an influence relation that shapes individual motivation in action in a certain way: the actions of individuals are motivated by group goals associated with the project they share."	Action, State
Montgomery 1961, 10	"The following definition ... : The capacity and the will to rally men and women to a common purpose, and the character which will inspire confidence."	Characteristic
Morris 2019, 21, 23	"Leadership ... An Influence process of the leader ... this phenomenon."	Action, Phenomenon
Morris 1969,* 743	"Leadership ... The position, office, or term of a leader ... A group of leaders ... The capacity to be a leader; ability to lead."	Characteristic, Role

Mumford, E. 1906, 218, 219, 221, 224, 229	"Leadership is a function common to … stages of the social process … whether the interactions be inter-individual, inter-groupal, or intra-groupal … one of the … general forms of association … the pre-eminence of one or a few individuals in a group in the process of control of societal phenomena … a phenomenon … a modal societal tendency. … classified among the … modal social tendencies or forces."	Action, Characteristic, Effect, Phenomenon, Role
Mumford, M. D. 2011, 1	"Leadership, the exercise of interpersonal influence … is a … form of performance—leadership does not exist unless something else happens."	Action, Effect
Mumford, M. D., Zaccaro, Connelly, and Marks 2000, 156	"Phenomena such as leadership."	Phenomenon
Mumford, M. D., Zaccaro, Harding, Jacobs, and Fleishman 2000, 11, 26	"Organizational leadership is a form of skilled performance … an interactional social phenomenon involving the exercise of influence and others' reactions to these influence attempts."	Action, Effect, Phenomenon
Munson 1921, 411–412	"Leadership elicits … obedience and cooperation from subordinates and is the antithesis of 'Prussian militarism.' … the creative and directive force of morale … the conductor which guides and transmits."	Action, Effect
Murphy, S. :E. and Johnson 2011, 461	"Leadership is … a type of social influence through which one successfully garners the help and support of others to achieve a common goal."	Effect

Murphy, S. E., Reichard, and Johnson 2008, 251	"Leadership is a social activity that includes both leaders and followers."	Action
Murray, Bradley, and Craigie 1908,* 144	"**Leadership** ... The dignity, office, or position of a leader, esp. of a political party; also, ability to lead."	Characteristic, Role
Murrell 1997, 35	"Leadership is a social act, a construction of a 'ship' as a collective vehicle to help take us where we as a group, organization or society desire to go ... components ... include leaders ... as well as the followers or supporters ... also ... the relationships between the two."	Action, Characteristic Concept, Role, State
Nahavandi 2009, 33	"Leadership is a social and an interpersonal process."	Action
Nanus 1989, 45, 50–52	"Leadership is a peculiar property of the human species ... healthy and creative deployment of oneself ... making people into effective collaborators in the important work of organizations, institutions, and society."	Action, Characteristic, Effect
Nazeemudeen 2019, 42	"Leadership is conceptualized within the definitional ambit of the following four thematic factors: position, person, result, and process."	Action, Effect, Role
Newcomb, Turner, and Converse 1965, 485	"Leadership is best understood as a role relationship in which one or more members are recognized as special facilitators toward group goals."	State
Nitze 1954, 377	"Leadership is the successful resolution of problems and the successful attainment of objectives which impress themselves as being important to those whom one is called upon to lead."	Effect

Northouse 1997, 3	"Phenomenon of leadership … *Leadership is a process whereby an individual influences a group of individuals to achieve a common goal.*"	Action, Phenomenon
Nye 2008, 19	"Leadership is the power to orient and mobilize others for a purpose."	Role
O'Connell 2014, 183	"Leadership is … a seminal applied skill."	Characteristic
Osborn and Hunt, J. G. 1975, 28	"Leadership is … discretionary influence … leader behaviors under the control of the leader … may vary from individual to individual (leader subordinate interactions which are not externally determined)."	Action
Osborn, Hunt, J. G. and Jauch 2002, 798, 803–805, 832	"Leadership is … the incremental influence of a boss toward subordinates … the collective incremental influence of leaders in and around the system … incremental influence of position holders exercised via direct and indirect means to maintain and/or alter the existing dynamics in and out of a system … a subjectively identifiable pattern of influence attempts … an emerging social construction embedded in a unique organization."	Action, Concept, Effect
Ospina and Hittleman 2011, 93	"Leadership … is the social and relational processes (meaning-making included) that emerge to address organizing and action."	Action
Ospina, Godsoe, Schall, and Dodge 2002, 59–60	"Leadership is perceived as a process in which people come together to pursue change."	Action

Padilla 2012, 3, 12	"Leadership is a process that … involves … the leader … also involves some followers and an organizational environment or context where leader-follower interactions occur. It is this leadership triangle—composed of leaders, followers and environments … Leadership is an organized group process with associated goals resulting in a set of outcomes."	Action, Concept, Effect
Paige 1977, 1–2	"'Political leadership' is the behavior or persons in positions of political authority, their competitors, and these both in interaction with other members of society … behavior of persons in positions of highest authority … also intermediate and lower levels … monarchs, presidents, and premiers … governors, provincial chairmen, and mayors, … village chiefs, headmen, and leaders of party cells … single personalities … also the 'collective leadership' of aggregate bodies … in interaction with 'followers.' … in (e.g., party, legislature, or bureaucracy) … or process (e.g., policy decision, election, or revolution) … across them all … men … women … incumbents … competitors … revolutionaries … those who rule by moral suasion and reasoned agreement … those who gain compliance by fear and force … the admirable but the despicable … the 'successful' … those who 'fail.'"	Action, Characteristic, Role

Perot 1993, as cited in McFarland, Senn, and Childress 1993, 73	"Leadership is empowering a group of people to successfully achieve a common goal."	Action
Perruci 2011, 83	"Leadership is the process by which leaders and followers develop a relationship and work together toward a goal (or goals) within an environmental context shaped by cultural values and norms."	Action
Peters and Austin 1985, 265	"Passion, care, intensity, consistency, attention, drama, of the implicit and explicit use of symbols— in short, of leadership."	Action, Characteristic
Peters and Waterman 1982, 82	"Leadership is ... is ... coalition building ... seeding of cabals ... in the bowels of the organization ... shifting the attention of the institution through the mundane language of management systems ... altering agendas so that new priorities get enough attention ... being visible when things are going awry, and invisible when they are working well ... building a loyal team at the top that speaks more or less with one voice ... listening carefully much of the time, ... speaking with encouragement, and reinforcing words with ... action ... being tough when necessary, and ... use of power.""	Action, Effect
Pfeffer 1977, 104	*"Leadership is a process of attributing causation to individual social actors."*	Action

Pfeffer 1978, 29–31	"Leadership, like other forms of social influence, is attributed by observers. Social action, in other words, has meaning only through some phenomenological process ... concept of leadership ... Leadership is the outcome of an attribution process in which observers—in order to achieve a feeling of control over their environment—tend to attribute outcomes to persons rather than to context, and the identification of individuals with leadership positions facilitates this attribution process."	Action, Concept, Effect
Phillips 1939, 49, 54–55	*Leadership*: The imposition, maintenance, and direction of moral unity to our ends."	Action
Pickett 2000,* 995	"**Leadership** ... The position or office of a leader ... Capacity or ability to lead ... A group of leaders ... Guidance; direction."	Action, Characteristic, Role

Pietraszewski 2020, 2–3, 6, 10, 12	"Leadership and followership is a … phenomenon … *Leadership and followership are best conceptualized … as evolved information-processing roles … that produce and maintain groups …* a set of information-processing roles … *central information-processing functions … 1: Creation of coalitions -* … generating and/or communicating … *2: Coalition execution and maintenance –* … having a mental representation of the coalition … maintaining … representations in others, directing and monitoring … behaviors and division of labor … monitoring motivation and investment … sanctioning … and orchestrating … responses … shifting the coalition's goals, and serving as the spokesperson … determining who is in good standing … and who is not … imagining and communicating what can be done … ability to create representations in the minds of others; … doing or saying something that captures the attention of others; to embody knowledge and skills that others incorporate into their own behavior; … responding to followership offerings and behaviors; and competing with rival instances of leadership information-processing."	Action, Characteristic, Phenomenon, Role
Pigors 1934, 378	"Leadership is a process of mutual stimulation which, by the successful interplay of relevant individual differences, controls human energy in the pursuit of a common cause."	Action

Pigors 1935, 16, 87, 200, 223, 241	"Leadership is a process of mutual stimulation which, by the successful interplay of relevant individual differences, controls human energy in the pursuit of a common cause … mutual stimulation of leader and followers … interstimulation … reciprocal leading and following … implies … the goal toward which both leader and follower consciously choose to progress … leadership is a … phenomenon."	Action, Concept, Effect, Phenomenon
Pondy 1978, 87	*Leadership is a Language Game … a form of social influence.*	Action, Effect
Porter, N. 1890,* 837	**Leadership** … The office of a leader.	Role
Prentice 1961, 143	"Leadership is the accomplishment of a goal through the direction of human assistants."	Effect
Pye 2005, 31	*Leadership as an example of sensemaking … a sensemaking process … in the daily doing of leading.*	Action
Raelin 2006, 156	"Leadership is a plural phenomenon."	Phenomenon
Rauch and Behling 1984, 46	"'Leadership' is … the process of influencing the activities of an organized group toward goal achievement."	Action
Rego, Mohono, and Peter 2019, 95	"Leadership is about relationships."	State
Reich 1993, as cited in McFarland, Senn, and Childress 1993, 189	"Leadership is a process, a set of attributes that stems … from the ability to wield formal authority … assert power … the ability to get people to listen and follow."	Action, Characteristic

Reiche, Bird, Mendenhall, and Osland 2017, 553, 554, 558, 565	"... leadership is a ... process ... emerging phenomena ... entails a process through which one person exerts influence over other individuals to guide, structure, and facilitate task completion and relationships in a collective ... involves influence on individuals, groups, and even organizational units ... involves certain activities and behaviors ... the leadership construct ... results in concept imprecision ... evolves and constitutes itself through interactions with other constituents."	Action, Concept, Effect, Phenomenon
Reuter 1941, 133	"**Leadership**. The control of many by a single person or by few individuals ... the relation of leadership."	Effect, State
Ridgeway 2003, 65	"Leadership is ... a ... phenomenon ... a consequence of the broader processes by which social hierarchies develop among people when they are oriented toward the accomplishment of a collective goal or task."	Effect, Phenomenon
Riggio 2008, 342	"**Leadership** as the ability to direct a group toward the attainment of goals."	Characteristic
Riggio 2011, 119–120	"*Leadership* refers to the higher-level functions of a person with authority or influence in a group—providing strategic direction, overseeing the decision-making process, initiating and managing change."	Action, Role
Robbins and Coulter 2003, 458, 666	"**Leadership** ... the process of influencing a group toward the achievement of goals ... **Leadership** The process of influencing a group toward the achievement of goals."	Action

Robbins and Coulter 2018, 555, 672	"**Leadership** is a process of leading a group and influencing that group to achieve its goals ... **Leadership** A process of influencing a group to achieve goals"	Action
Rodgers and Bligh 2014, 28	"Leadership is a process grounded in the relationship between leader and follower."	Action
Rooney and Soukhanov 2004,* 1071	"**Leadership** ... **ABILITY TO LEAD** The ability to guide, direct, or influence people ... **GUIDANCE** guidance or direction ... **LEADERS** a group of leaders (takes a singular or plural verb) ... **OFFICE OR POSITION OF LEADER** the office or position of the head of a political party or other body of people"	Action, Characteristic, Role
Rost 1991, xiv, 102, 111, 116, 159	"Concept of leadership ... Leadership is an influence relationship among leaders and followers who intend real changes that reflect their mutual purposes ... Leadership is the sum total of all the interactions among all the leaders and followers in that relationship ... there must be more than one follower ... Leadership happens when leaders and followers enter into a relationship that intends real changes ... a process oriented to changing organizations and societies."	Action, Concept, State

Rost 1993, 99–101, 103	"Leadership is an influence relationship among leaders and their collaborators who intend real changes that reflect their mutual purposes ... leaders and their collaborators influence one another about real changes that reflect their mutual purposes ... what the leaders and collaborators do together to change organizations ... takes place during a specific change process ... an episode in people's lives."	Action, State
Rost 2008, 61	"Leadership is an episodic series of activities through which people develop a relationship to make significant changes ... episodic nature of the dynamic that is leadership."	Action
Rost and Barker 2000, 5, 10	"Leadership is a socially constructed reality ... a dynamic political relationship ... The concept of leadership ... leadership is a process of change that occurs ... a temporal property of the actor."	Action, Characteristic, Concept, State
Ruben and Gigliotti 2017, 17–18	"Leadership is ... a communicative process ... extends beyond the role of titular leader ... lies at the intersection of science and art ... As an art ... leadership is ... a personal phenomenon."	Action, Characteristic, Phenomenon
Saghal and Pathak 2007, 279	"Leadership is a lifetime process."	Action
Salovaara and Ropo 2013, 198	"Leadership, being a quality of an organization and its culture ... a socially constructed and emerging phenomenon ... and as meaning making (Smircich & Morgan, 1982) ... an aesthetic and embodied phenomenon."	Action, Characteristic, Phenomenon

Sarkesian 1981, 243	"Leadership means to inspire others to undertake some form of purposeful action as determined by the leader."	Effect
Schein 1985, xi	"Leadership—the ability to see a need for change and the ability to make it happen."	Characteristic
Schenk 1928, 111	"Leadership is the management of men by persuasion and inspiration … the art of leading … It implies followship."	Action, Characteristic
Seeman 1960, 127	"Leadership … as 'acts by persons which influence other persons in a shared direction.'"	Action
Senge 2016, as cited in Schuyler 2016, 67	**"Leadership is the capacity of a human community to shape its future."**	Characteristic
Shamir, 2004, 503	"Leadership is a relationship that is jointly produced by leaders and followers."	State
Shaw 1981, 295, 317	"Leadership is a special case of social influence; that is, leadership is the exercise of power in particular situations, as by the occupant of a particular position in the group structure … a process … an influence process which is directed toward goal achievement."	Action, Effect
Sher 2004, 1265	"Leadership is the ability of people to use every aspect of experience for thinking through or offering new insights into the situations they are in."	Characteristic

Shore 2014, 188–189	"Political leadership is a process of continuous contestation and negotiation fought over what are largely symbolic grounds ... the art of winning and controlling followers, which, ... requires the strategic uses of morality and successful mobilization of rituals and symbols."	Action, Characteristic
Silva 2016, 3	*"Leadership is the process of interactive influence that occurs when, in a given context, some people accept someone as their leader to achieve common goals."*	Action
Simpson and Weiner 1989/1991,* 750	"**Leadership** ... The dignity, office, or position of a leader, esp. of a political party; ability to lead; the position of a group of people leading or influencing others within a given context; the group itself; the action or influence necessary for the direction or organization of effort in a group undertaking."	Action, Characteristic, Effect, Role
Slatter 1984, 148	"Leadership ... is a concept ... giving a sense of direction by setting priorities and short-term goals; establishing a sense of urgency; defining responsibilities; resolving conflict; conveying enthusiasm and dedication; and giving credit where it is due and rewarding it accordingly."	Action, Concept, Effect

Smircich and Morgan 1982, 257–259, 261	"The concept of leadership ... the phenomenon of leadership ... realized in the process whereby one or more individuals succeeds in attempting to frame and define the reality of others ... phenomena ... socially constructed ... emerging as a result of the constructions and actions of both leaders and led ... a complicity or process of negotiation ... a social process defined through interaction ... involves ... defining reality in ways that are sensible to the led ... a dependency relationship in which individuals surrender their powers to interpret and define reality to others ... an additional stage of institutionalization, in which rights and obligations to define the nature of experience and activity are recognized and formalized ... identifiable ... as a form of action that seeks to shape its context."	Action, Concept, Effect, Phenomenon, State
Solomon 1993, as cited in McFarland, Senn, and Childress 1993, 102–103	"Leadership is the fulfillment of a vision through others."	Action

Sorial 2015, 84, 92	"Leadership is ... assuming responsibility for a social co-ordination problem in an ethical way; and ... a leader ... who can convince others that this is, in fact, the best way of acting in the given circumstances." "The concept of leadership ... the phenomenon of leadership ... realized in the process whereby one or more individuals succeeds in attempting to frame and define the reality of others ... phenomena ... socially constructed ... emerging as a result of the constructions and actions of both leaders and led ... a complicity or process of negotiation ... a social process defined through interaction ... involves ... defining reality in ways that are sensible to the led ... a dependency relationship in which individuals surrender their powers to interpret and define reality to others ... an additional stage of institutionalization, in which rights and obligations to define the nature of experience and activity are recognized and formalized ... identifiable ... as a form of action that seeks to shape its context."	Action, Characteristic
Soukhanov 1992,* 1023	"**Leadership ...** The position or office of a leader ... Capacity or ability to lead ... A group of leaders ... Guidance; direction."	Action, Characteristic, Role

Springborg 2010, 246–247, 256	"What is leadership? … making sure (profitable) decisions are made and followed up by efficient action … decisions … based on the way the leader (influenced by or collaborating with the board, the team, and customers/ users) makes sense of the situation … How do we make sure that the assumptions embedded in the way we make sense of things do not remove the best possibilities and leave us with a range of mediocre possibilities to choose from? … an art … an arrangement of conditions (workspaces, composition of teams, meeting agendas, etc.) in such a way that the composition will give spectators (employees, leaders, managers, boardmembers, etc.) the opportunity of perceiving elements of their work life (for instance, daily tasks, collaborations, other departments, other organizations, the management team) more directly through their senses."""	Action, Characteristic, Concept
Stainton Rogers 2011, 372	"Leadership is about the ability to influence others, in ways relevant to the contexts (such as in politics or management)."	Characteristic
Stech 2008, 48	"Leadership … a state or condition within an individual and … the exhibition or embodiment of the quality or state of leadership in action."	Action, State
Stein and Urdang 1966,* 814	"**Leadership** … the position or function of a leader … ability to lead … an act or instance of leading … the leaders of a group."	Action, Characteristic, Role

Stewart 1927, as cited in Moore 1927, 124	"General Stewart defined leadership as the ability to impress the will of the leader on those led and induce obedience, respect, loyalty, and cooperation."	Characteristic
Stogdill 1950, 4	"Leadership may be considered as the process (act) of influencing the activities of an organized group in its efforts towards goal setting and goal achievement."	Action
Stogdill 1974, 7, 411	"Leadership appears to be a ... concept ... Leadership is defined as the initiation and maintenance of structure in expectation and interaction ... Leadership is an aspect of role differentiation in a group."	Action, Concept, Role
Sturm and Monzani 2010, 275	"Leadership is a process that involves personal characteristics of the leader, the interaction between the leader and follower(s), and situational pressures."	Action, Characteristic
Tannenbaum, R., Weschler, and Massarik 1961, 24–29, 426	"We define leadership as *interpersonal influence, exercised in situation and directed, through the communication process, toward the attainment of a specified goal or goals.* ... always involves attempts on the part of a *leader* (influencer), to affect (influence) the behavior of a *follower* (influencee) or followers in a *situation* ... a *process* or *function*."	Action, Effect
Tead 1927, as cited in Moore 1927, 124	"Ordway Tead ... stated that the newer ideal of leadership ... is replacing the feudal concept of leadership. The new ideal conceives leadership as successful in so far as the ends of the ones lead are identified with the ends of the leader."	Concept, Effect

Tead 1929, 149	"Leadership is the name for that combination of qualities by the possession of which one is able to get something done by others chiefly because through his influence they become willing to do it. It is ability to secure *willing* action in behalf of an established purpose."	Characteristic
Tead 1935, 20	"Leadership is the activity of influencing people to cooperate toward some goal which they come to find desirable."	Characteristic
Thoroughgood, Sawyer, Padilla, and Lunsford 2016, 628	"The term 'leadership' ... reflects a dynamic, cocreated process between leaders, followers, and the environment."	Action
Ulmer 2017, 5	"Organizational leadership is 'a process in which an individual provides direction, motivation, and resources to accomplish a mission.'"	Action
Underdal 1994, 178, 181	"Leadership ... as an asymmetrical relationship of influence in which one actor guides or directs the behavior of others toward a certain goal over a certain period of time."	State
Urwich 1961, 426	"The active form of the verb 'to lead' is *leading.* To lead means to go in front of, be ahead of, guide ... leadership is the kind of behavior which enables an individual to lead others. It may be defined formally as *the kind of behavior by an individual which inclines others to accept his/her guidance.*"	Action
Van Vugt 2006, 355	"Leadership ... a process of influence to attain mutual goals."	Action
Van Vugt 2012, 142	"Leadership ... a process of influence to achieve coordination between individuals for the pursuit of mutual goals."	Action

Van Vugt 2018, 192	"Leadership ... a process of influence over the establishment of goals, logistics of coordination, monitoring of effort, and reward or punishment strategies."	Action
Van Vugt, Hogan, R., and Kaiser 2008, 182–183	"Leadership ... influencing individuals to contribute to group goals and ... coordinating the pursuit of those goals ... building a team and guiding it to victory ... a resource for groups and an attribute of individuals."	Action, Characteristic, Concept, Effect
Varney 2009, 5	"Leadership ... the ability to create a field of meaning."	Characteristic
Vizetelly 1922,* 654	"**Leadership** ... office of a leader; guidance."	Action, Role
Von Rueden and Van Vugt 2015, 978	"Leadership is a primary mechanism by which groups resolve coordination and motivation problems."	Action
Vroom and Jago 2007, 17–18	"Leadership ... refers to a potential or capacity to influence others ... represented in ... a process that includes the traits of the source of the influence ... the cognitive processes in the source ... the nature of the interaction that makes the influence possible ... and the situational context ... a process of motivating people to work together collaboratively to accomplish great things ... involves ... influence called *motivating*."	Action, Characteristic, Effect
Waldman and O'Reilly 2020, 4	"**Leadership** the process of exerting intentional influence toward the ideas, beliefs/values, capabilities, and behaviors of others, willingly on their part, toward an organizational goal(s) or vision."	Action
Walker and Aritz 2014, 14	"Leadership is defined as the ability to influence a group toward the achievement of goals."	Characteristic

Walsh, Jamison, and Walsh 2009, 99, 117	"Leadership is expertise … skills … the ability to listen."	Characteristic
Walters 2009, 90	*"Leadership deals with the ability of a person generally in a precedent position to provide others with the guidance necessary to influence them to act in a certain way or move in a specific direction* … conceptualization of leadership … position, ability, and influence are all … essential elements."	Characteristic, Concept, Effect, Role
Watkins 1989, 27	"Leadership as a dialectic relationship … a social construction of reality which involves an ongoing interaction."	Concept, State
Webster and Goodrich 1847/1848,* 653	"**LEADERSHIP** … state or condition of a leader."	State
Webster's Collegiate Dictionary 1916,* 564	"**Leadership** … Office, position, or dignity of a leader; also, ability to lead."	Characteristic, Role
Weiss 2011, 2	"**Leadership** is the ability to influence followers to achieve common goals through shared purposes."	Characteristic
Whitney 1889–1891,* 3385	"**Leadership** … The office of a leader; guidance; control."	Action, Effect, Role
Wilson 2016, 2	"Leadership … is … a *social invention* … something malleable … we can (re-)form in a manner which reflects *our* priorities and *our* values."	Characteristic, Concept
Wilson, O'Hare, and Shipper 1990, 185	"Leadership is … one of several organizational roles that depend on skills at influencing others."	Role
Wooden 2007, 184, 191	"Leadership is a trust … power."	Characteristic, Role

Woolf 1973,* 653	"**Leadership** ... the office or position of a leader ... the quality of a leader: capacity to lead."	Characteristic, Role
Worcester 1846,* 413	"**LEADERSHIP** ... The office of a leader."	Role
Worcester 1860,* 823	"**LEADERSHIP** ... The state or the office of a leader."	Role, State
Wren 2011, 70	"Leadership ... a dynamic and context-bound relationship among individuals."	State
Wren and Price 2007, 215	"Leadership ... as a mutual influence process among leaders and followers in which each participant harbors his or her own complex motives and constructions of reality and operates as part of a collective in a complicated and ever-shifting environment in an effort to achieve desired goals."	Action
Yammarino 2013, 150, 154	"*Leadership is a multi-level (person, dyad, group, collective) leader-follower interaction process that occurs in a particular situation (context) where a leader (e.g., superior, supervisor) and followers (e.g., subordinates, direct reports) share a purpose (vision, mission) and jointly accomplish things (e.g., goals, objectives, tasks) willingly (e.g., without coercion)* ... a ... phenomenon involving numerous constructs, processes, and entities (e.g., individuals, dyads, groups and teams, and various collectives such as organizations, networks, and multiteam systems)."	Action, Concept, Phenomenon, Role

Young 1991, 281, 285	"Leadership is ... a complex phenomenon ... refers to the actions of individuals who endeavor to solve or circumvent the collective action problems that plague the efforts of parties seeking to reap joint gains in processes of institutional bargaining."	Action, Phenomenon
Yukl 1989a, 5	"Leadership ... a ... phenomenon ... defined ... to include influence processes involving determination of the group's or organization's objectives, motivating task behavior in pursuit of these objectives, and influencing group maintenance and culture."	Action, Effect, Phenomenon
Yukl 1989b, 253	"Leadership ... a ... phenomenon ... defined ... to include influencing task objectives and strategies, influencing commitment and compliance in task behavior to achieve these objectives, influencing group maintenance and identification, and influencing the culture of an organization."	Effect, Phenomenon
Yukl 1994, 5	"Leadership ... phenomenon ... viewed ... as influence processes affecting the interpretation of events for followers, the choice of objectives for the group or organization, the organization of work activities to accomplish the objectives, the motivation of followers to achieve the objectives, the maintenance of cooperative relationships and teamwork, and the enlistment of support and cooperation from people outside the group or organization."	Action, Phenomenon

Yukl 1998, 5	"Leadership ... a ... phenomenon ... viewed ... as the process wherein an individual member of a group or organization influences the interpretation of events, the choice of objectives and strategies, the organization of work activities, the motivation of people to achieve the objectives, the maintenance of cooperative relationships, the development of skills and confidence by members, and the enlistment of support and cooperation from people outside the group or organization."	Action, Phenomenon
Yukl 2002, 6–7	"Like all constructs in social science ... Leadership ... a ... phenomenon ... Leadership is the process of influencing others to understand and agree about what needs to be done and how it can be done effectively, and the process of facilitating individual and collective efforts to accomplish the shared objectives."	Action, Concept Phenomenon
Yukl 2006, 8	"Leadership ... a ... phenomenon ... Leadership is the process of influencing others to understand and agree about what needs to be done and how to do it, and the process of facilitating individual and collective efforts to accomplish shared objectives."	Action, Phenomenon

Yukl and Van Fleet 1992, 149	"Leadership is viewed as a process that includes influencing the task objectives and strategies of a group or organization, influencing people in the organization to implement the strategies and achieve the objectives, influencing group maintenance and identification, and influencing the culture of the organization."	Action
Zastrow and Kirst-Ashman 2001, 354–355	"*Leadership* means one member is influencing other group members to help the group reach its goals ... the performance of acts that help the group reach its goals and maintain itself in good working order."	Action, Effect
Zhou, Wang, and Vancouver 2019, 405	"More than ... a personal trait of those individuals assigned to leadership roles, leadership is a dynamic process that unfolds over time under the joint influence of internal performance states, exogenous shocks from external performance environment, and work design factors."	Action, Characteristic

* Popular dictionary

Table 2. Words or Phrases Interpreted within Context of Use

Action	abilities used
	act
	action
	actions
	activities
	activities of many organized
	activity
	acts
	aligning people
	aligning resources
	an experience
	assuming responsibility
	attempt to influence
	attempts
	attempts of change of behavior
	attention
	behaving
	behavior
	behaviors
	being tough
	being visible
	bringing people together
	building a team
	building purpose
	building teams
	challenging
	cognitive processes
	communicating
	communication
	communication of idea
	competing
	complicity of negotiation
	conductor that guides

conductor that transmits

consistency

consolidating attention

construct patterns

conveying dedication

conveying enthusiasm

coordinating

coordinating work

creating patterns

defining

defining responsibility

deployment

deployment of oneself

design

development

development of idea

direct

directing

direction

discretionary influence of leader behaviors

does

doing

drama

dynamic

earn trust

effort

embodiment of quality in action

embodiment of state in action

empowering

enabling

encourage

encouragement

endeavor

ensuring decisions are profitable

episode

establishing

establishing direction

example of sensemaking

exchange of information

exchange of resources

exercise of power

exhibition of quality in action

exhibition of state in action

expression of power

face-to-face contact

factor of process

fair dealings

finding people

force of morale

force of society

formulation of vision

fulfillment of a vision

function

game of language

gives support for behavior

gives support for creative ways of doing things

giving credit

giving direction

giving directions

going out ahead

governance

guidance

guiding

guiding team to victory

imagining

imitating

impartation of convictions

imposition

inducing followers

influencing work

initiating

initiation of structure

instance

instances

interact

interacting

interaction

interactions

interplay of attitudes

journey

judge

listening

maintaining

maintenance

maintenance of structure

management

managing

manifestation of perceiving

manifested

marshalling of power capabilities and material resources

meaning making

meaning-making

means

mechanism

mobilize

mobilizing

obtaining

orchestrating conflicts

ordering of priorities

organization of activities

organizing work

others' reactions

overseeing decision-making

part of locomotion of group

part of management

part of problem-solving

pattern of actions

pattern of attempts

penalize

performance

problem-solving

process

process of negotiation

processes

protecting

provides encouragement

provides shelter for risking

provides shelter for venturing

providing direction

providing direction

reactions

recognition of need

resources used

responding

reward

rewarding

say

saying

says

science

seeding cabals

seek out

series of activities

series of acts

service

set agenda

set of practices

set of processes

setting goals

setting up patterns

show the way

something we say

speaking

stage of institutionalization

stimuli

strategy

structure in social process of patterns of social interaction

structure of actions

tactics

taking care nothing will split up attention

techniques

tending to fitness

tending to growth

tending to innovation

tending to the future of organizations

thinking

thinks

tool

transaction

trying to influence

uncovering and exploiting

unsuccessful attempts

use of capabilities

use of incentives

use of power

use of symbols

utilizing

valuing people

way actors experience processes

way of thinking

ways leadership exerted

ways of acting

what a person does

wielding of power

	words
	work
Characteristic	abilities
	ability
	able
	art
	aspect of human life
	capacity
	character
	characteristics
	commitment
	competence
	component of leaders
	constraints
	control of temper
	conviction
	courage
	curiosity
	daring
	dedication
	definitional feature of leader's dispositional characteristics
	determination
	dignity
	disposition
	dynamic of staying power
	dynamic of values
	dynamic of vision
	element of intellect
	element of power
	element of sociability
	embody knowledge incorporated by others
	embody skills incorporated by others
	essence
	experiences
	expertise

explanation

extra something

facet of process

factor

factors

feature

foresight

genius

humility

increment over and above compliance

initiative

inseparable from followers' needs and goals

insistence

integrity

intensity

know what to do

knowledge

leader who can convince others

matter of how to be

name for qualities

network-property

opportunities

passion

perseverance

personalities of people

personality

potential

power

power of ability

power of knowledge

pressures of situation

principles

property

purpose

qualities

	quality
	resource for groups
	responsibility
	self-reliance
	sense of what should be done
	set of abilities
	set of attributes
	set of skills
	sincerity
	situation
	situational context
	skill
	skills
	something malleable
	steadfastness of purpose
	steadiness
	talents
	tenacity
	tendency of society
	the person
	trait
	traits
	trust
	understanding
	vision
	will
Concept	abstraction
	an overlay
	attribute
	attribution
	attributions
	behaviors interpreted by followers
	being perceived as leader
	being seen as leader
	can be used to understand production of set of outcomes

can be used to understand production of state of affairs

caring about task to be done

caring about welfare of others

category of explanation

characteristics interpreted by followers

conceived

concept

conception

conceptual

conceptualization

construct

construction

construction by followers

construction of reality

constructs

enrichment of conceptualization of relationship

ensure possibilities are best

expectation

explanation

explanation used to understand organizations

fulcrum

goal

goals

ideology

interpretation by followers

interpretations

invention

label

locates reasons

making sense

outcomes interpreted by followers

perceived

perception

perception of another

perception of others

	reality
	reality defined
	reality framed
	representation of influence
	representations
	resides in eyes of the follower
	result of process
	state of mind of followers
	theories of good leadership
	traits interpreted by followers
	triangle
	tripod
	understanding
	used to understand organizations
	vehicle of collective
	views about characteristics
	views of reality
	what followers think
Effect	acceptance
	accomplishment of goal
	acquisition of help
	acquisition of support
	action endorsed
	adapted
	adoption of goals
	agent of control
	altering agendas
	antecedent and interstimulation
	antithesis of militarism
	attainment of objectives
	attempt of influence viewed as legitimate
	benefit
	building coalition
	building personality
	building teams of loyalty

causing willing effort

change

change consistent with goals of other

change generated

changing

communicating vision internalized by others

communication accepted freely

communication adhered to

communication internalized

communication received positively

consequence

control

control of phenomena

cooperation

course of action of many changed

creating effective collaborators

direction accepted

effect

effects

ends of followers identified with ends of leaders

energizing people

engaging

establishing urgency

exercise of influence

exerting influence

exertion of influence

factor of result

forging vision internalized by others

function

function of complexity of context

function of leader

function of led

get others to want to do what is to be done

imitation

impact on system of beliefs

increment of influence

increment over and above formal prescription

influence

influence exerted

influence extra

influences

influencing

inspire others

inspiring people

interstimulation

leading

lifting vision

maintaining ideas, beliefs, morale,
values, and understandings

make others serve a common purpose

modification of competence

modification of motivation

modifies attitudes and behaviors of others

motivating

motivating work

mutual stimulation of leader and followers

obedience

other convinced personal future will be
better if behaves appropriately

outcome

outcome of processes

outcomes

performance

persuading

persuasion

phenomenon of influence

power of personal liking

produced

product

raising performance

	recipient convinced of benefit
	reciprocal following
	reciprocal leading
	resolution of problems
	resolving conflict
	response
	result
	result of effort above and beyond norm of role
	result of effort above and beyond requirement of position
	result of infusion of values
	result of occurrence
	result of process
	revising ideas, beliefs, morale, values, and understandings
	secure satisfying performance
	shaping ideas, values, perceptions, and feelings
	shifting attention
	solutions
	something happening as a result
	stimulation that causes a number of people to set out toward an old goal with new zest or a new goal with hopeful courage
	stimulation that controls human energy in pursuit of cause
	strengthening ideas, beliefs, morale, values, and understandings
	those influenced
	transformation of doubts
	willingness of follower to forgo self-interest
	willingness of follower to make sacrifices
Phenomenon	aesthetic and embodied phenomenon
	complex phenomenon
	complex, multifaceted phenomenon
	complex, multilevel phenomena
	consequential phenomenon
	daily and fluctuating phenomenon
	emergent phenomenon
	group phenomenon

	interactional phenomenon
	interactional social phenomenon
	leadership phenomenon
	novel, emerging phenomena
	one of the most complex and multifaced phenomena
	organizational phenomenon
	personal phenomenon
	pervasive and decentralized phenomenon
	phenomena
	phenomenon
	plural phenomenon
	psychological phenomenon
	relational phenomenon
	seldom spectacular phenomenon
	social phenomenon
	socially constructed and emerging phenomenon
Role	ability to exert authority
	aspect of role differentiation
	association
	authority
	competitors of people in positions of authority
	component of followers: role
	component of role
	component of supporters
	dominance
	element of power
	elements of coercion:
	entities of collectives (organizations, networks, systems of teams)
	entities of dyads
	entities of groups
	entities of individuals
	entities of teams
	factor of person
	factor of position

followers
fulfilling authority
function
functions
group
group of leaders
group of persons
groups of people in positions of authority
headship
in charge
job
leader
leaders
office
others
people in positions of authority
position
power
power
power of position
preeminence of a few
preeminence of one
requirement of job
requirement of systems
responsibility
role
role-inherent
roles
set of functions
sources of power
status
system that encourages compliance
system that encourages feeling leader can
create problems for followers
system that encourages respect

	term
	vertical social distance
State	bond of leaders and constituents
	condition
	part of duality
	part of relationship
	relation
	relationship
	state
	state of mind of followers
	system of relationships

Table 3. Classifications of 713 Popular-Dictionary
and Nondictionary Definitions of Leadership
as Interpreted in 381 Publications

Classifications	Number	Percent of 381 Publications
Action	266	69.8
Characteristic	121	31.8
Concept	62	16.3
Effect	100	26.2
Phenomenon	54	14.2
Role	67	17.6
State	43	11.3

Table 4. Classifications of 70 Popular-Dictionary Definitions of Leadership as Interpreted in 27 Publications

Classifications	Number	Percent of 27 Publications
Action	17	63.0
Characteristic	21	77.8
Concept	0	0.0
Effect	3	11.1
Phenomenon	0	0.0
Role	26	96.3
State	3	11.1

Table 5. Classifications of 643 Nondictionary Definitions of Leadership as Interpreted in 354 Publications

Classifications	Number	Percent of 354 Publications
Action	249	70.3
Characteristic	100	28.2
Concept	62	17.5
Effect	97	27.4
Phenomenon	54	15.3
Role	41	11.6
State	40	11.3

Table 6. Comparison of Percentages of Classifications of 713 Leadership Definitions in 27 Popular-Dictionary and 354 Nondictionary Publications as Interpreted in 381 Publications

Classifications	Percent of 27 Popular-Dictionary Publications	Percent of 354 Nondictionary Publications
Action	63.0	70.3
Characteristic	77.8	28.2
Concept	0.0	17.5
Effect	11.1	27.4
Phenomenon	0.0	15.3
Role	96.3	11.6
State	11.1	11.3

Table 7. Classifications of Popular-Dictionary Definitions of Leadership as Interpreted in 27 Publications by Time Period

Classifi-cations	Number in Period 1846–1899	Percent of 6 Pub-lications	Number by Period 1900–1951	Percent of 6 Pub-lications	Number by Period 1952–2004	Percent of 15 Pub-lications
Action	2	33.3	4	66.7	11	73.3
Charac-teristic	1	16.7	5	83.3	15	100.0
Concept	0	0.0	0	0.0	0	0.0
Effect	1	16.7	0	0.0	2	13.3
Pheno-menon	0	0.0	0	0.0	0	0.0
Role	5	83.3	6	100.0	15	100.0
State	2	33.3	0	0.0	1	6.7

Table 8. Classifications of Nondictionary Definitions of Leadership as Interpreted in 354 Publications by Time Period

Time Period	Number of Publications	Action	Characteristic	Concept	Effect	Phenomenon	Role	State
1900–1919	4	2	3	0	2	1	1	0
	Percent of 4 Publications	50.0	75.0	0.0	50.0	25.0	25.0	0.0
1920–1929	15	6	8	1	6	2	1	0
	Percent of 15 Publications	40.0	53.3	6.7	40.0	13.3	6.7	0.0
1930–1939	9	5	6	1	3	2	1	0
	Percent of 9 Publications	55.6	66.7	11.1	33.3	22.2	11.1	0.0
1940–1949	9	6	1	1	2	2	1	3
	Percent of 9 Publications	66.7	11.1	11.1	22.2	22.2	11.1	33.3
1950–1959	9	6	1	1	4	1	1	0
	Percent of 9 Publications	66.7	11.1	11.1	44.4	11.1	11.1	0.0
1960–1969	28	15	8	7	10	4	3	7
	Percent of 28 Publications	53.6	28.6	25.0	35.7	14.3	10.7	25.0

Time Period	Number of Publications	Action	Characteristic	Concept	Effect	Phenomenon	Role	State
1970–1979	25	24	7	9	6	2	3	2
	Percent of 25 Publications	96.0	28.0	36.0	24.0	8.0	12.0	8.0
1980–1989	32	23	10	6	10	5	5	3
	Percent of 32 Publications	71.9	31.3	18.8	31.3	15.6	15.6	9.4
1990–1999	44	33	9	8	12	8	8	7
	Percent of 44 Publications	75.0	20.5	18.2	27.3	18.2	18.2	15.9
2000–2009	83	58	23	15	19	14	8	12
	Percent of 83 Publications	69.9	27.7	18.1	22.9	16.9	9.6	14.5
2010–2020	96	71	24	13	23	13	9	6
	Percent of 96 Publications	74.0	25.0	13.5	24.0	13.5	9.4	6.3

BIBLIOGRAPHY

Allport, F. I I. 1964. *Social Psychology*. New York: Johnson Reprint. Original work published 1924.

Alvesson, M. 2020. "Upbeat Leadership: A Recipe for—or against—"Successful" Leadership Studies." *The Leadership Quarterly* 31, no. 6: 1–12. https://doi.org/10.1016/j.leaqua.2020.101439.

Alvesson, M., and Spicer, A. 2014. "Critical Perspectives on Leadership." In D. V. Day ed., *The Oxford Handbook of Leadership and Organization*, 40–56. New York: Oxford University Press.

Andersen, J. A. 2014. "Ladies and Gentlemen: Leadership Has Left the Building." *Leadership and the Humanities* 2, no. 2: 94–107.

Andriessen, E. J. H., and Drenth, P. J. D. 1984 "Leadership: Theories and Models." In P. J. D. Drenth, H. Thierry, P. J. Willems, and C. J. de Wolff, eds., *Handbook of Work and Organizational Psychology*, 1:481–520. Chichester: John Wiley and Sons.

Atkins, B. T. S., and Rundell, M. 2008. *The Oxford Guide to Practical Lexicography*. New York: Oxford University Press.

Antonakis, J., and Atwater, L. 2002. "Leader Distance: A Review and a Proposed Theory." *The Leadership Quarterly* 13, no. 6: 673–704.

Antonakis, J.; Cianciolo, A. T.; and Sternberg, R. J. 2004. "Leadership: Past, Present, and Future." In J. Antonakis, A. T. Cianciolo, and R. J. Sternberg, eds., *The Nature of Leadership*, 3–15. Thousand Oaks, CA: SAGE.

Antonakis, J., and Day, D. V. 2018. "Leadership: Past, Present, and Future." In J. Antonakis and D. V. Day, eds., *The Nature of Leadership*, 3rd ed., 3–26. Thousand Oaks, CA: SAGE.

Archives at Yale. n.d. "Goodrich Family Papers" Retrieved January 31, 2022. https://archives.yale.edu/repositories/12/resources/3046.

Arvey, R. D.; Wang, N.; Song, Z.; and Li, W. 2014. "The Biology of Leadership." In D. V. Day, ed., *The Oxford Handbook of Leadership and Organization*, 73–90. New York: Oxford University Press.

Ashford, S. J., and DeRue, D. S. 2012. "Developing as a Leader: The Power of Mindful Engagement." *Organizational Dynamics* 41:146–154.

Atwater, L. E.; and Yammarino, F. J. 1992. "Does Self-Other Agreement on Leadership Perceptions Moderate the Validity of Leadership and Performance Predictions?" *Personnel Psychology* 45, no. 1: 141–164.

Avolio, B. J. 2007. Promoting more integrative strategies for leadership theory-building. *American Psychologist, 62*(1), 25-33.

Bailey, N. 1727. *The Universal Etymological English Dictionary*, Vol. 2. Printed for T. Cox.

Baker, S. D. 2006. The Effect of Leader-Follower Agreement on Team Effectiveness. Doctoral dissertation, George Washington University. ProQuest Dissertations.

Baker, S. D.; Anthony, E. L.; and Stites-Doe, S. A. 2015. "Most Admired Leader/Most Admired Follower." *Organization Management Journal* 12, no. 1: 23–33.

Baliga, B. R., and Hunt, J. C. 1988. "An Organizational Life Cycle Approach to Leadership." In J. C. Hunt, B. R. Baliga, H. R. Dacher, and C. A. Schriesheim, eds., *Emerging Leadership Vistas*, 129–149. Lexington, MA: D. C. Health.

Bann, C. L. 2007. "Entrepreneurial Lives: A Phenomenological Study of the Lived Experience of the Entrepreneur, Including the Influence of Values, Beliefs, Attitudes, and Leadership in the Entrepreneurial Journey." Doctoral dissertation, Capella University. ProQuest Dissertations.

Barge, J. K., and Fairhurst, G. 2008. "Living Leadership: A Systemic Constructionist Approach." *Leadership Quarterly* 4, no. 3: 227–251.

Barker, R. A. 2001. "The Nature of Leadership." *Human Relations* 54, no. 4: 469–494.

Barker, R. A. 2002. *On the Nature of Leadership*. Lanham, MD: University Press of America.

Barnard, C. I. 1938. *The Functions of the Executive*. Cambridge, MA: Harvard University Press.

Barnard, C. I. 1948. *Organization and Management: Selected Papers*. Cambridge, MA: Harvard University Press.

Barnhart, C. L., ed. 1947. *American College Dictionary*. New York: Random House.

Barnhart, C. L., ed. 1963. *The World Book Encyclopedia Dictionary*. New York: Random House.

Barrow, J. C. 1977. "The Variables of Leadership." *Academy of Management Review* 2, no. 2: 231–251.

Bass, B. M. 1960. *Leadership, Psychology, and Organizational Behavior*. New York: Harper and Brothers.

Bass, B. M. 1981. *Stogdill's Handbook of Leadership: A Survey of Theory and Research*, rev. ed. New York: Free.

Bass, B. M. 1990. *Bass and Stogdill's Handbook of Leadership: Theory, Research, and Managerial Applications*, 3rd ed. New York: Free.

Bass, B. M. 1998. "The Ethics of Transformational Leadership." In J. B. Ciulla, ed., *Ethics, The Heart of Leadership*, 169–192. Westport, CN: Quorum.

Bass, B. M., and Bass, R. 2008. *The Bass Handbook of Leadership: Theory, Research, and Managerial Applications*, 4th ed. New York: Free.

Bastardoz, N., and Van Vugt, M. 2019. "The Nature of Followership: Evolutionary Analysis and Review." *Leadership Quarterly* 30, no. 1: 81–95.

Bavelas, A. 1960. "Leadership: Man and Function." *Administrative Science Quarterly* 4, no. 4: 491–498.

Beal, G. M., Bohlen, J. M., and Raudabaugh, J. N. 1962. *Leadership and Dynamic Group Action*. Ames: Iowa State University Press.

Bejoint, H. 2010. *The Lexicography of English: From Origins to Present*. New York: Oxford University Press.

Bennis, W. G. 1959. "Leadership Theory and Administrative Behavior: The Problem with Authority." *Administrative Science Quarterly* 4, no. 3: 295–301.

Bennis, W. G. 1961. "Revisionist Theory of Leadership." *Harvard Business Review* 39, no. 1: 26–28, 31, 34, 36, 146, 148, 150.

Bennis, W. G. 1989. *On Becoming a Leader*. Reading, MA: Addison-Wesley.

Bennis, W. G. 2007. "The Challenges of Leadership in the Modern World." *American Psychologist* 62:1, 2–5.

Bingham, W. V. 1927. "Leadership." In H. C. Metcalf, ed., *The Psychological Foundations of Management*, 244–260. Chicago: A. W. Shaw.

Birnbaum, R. 2013. "Genes, Memes, and the Evolution of Human Leadership." In M. G. Ramsey, ed., *The Oxford Handbook of Leadership*, 243–266. New York: Oxford University Press.

Blackmar, F. W. 1911. "Leadership in Reform." *American Journal of Sociology* 16, no. 3: 626–644.

Blanchard, K. H. 2010. *Leading at a Higher Level: Blanchard on Leadership and Creating High Performing Organizations*. Mason, OH: FT.

Blondel, J. 1987. *Political Leadership: Toward a General Analysis*. London: SAGE.

Blount, T. 1972. *Glossographia*, 2nd ed. Printed for Tho. Newcombe for George Sawbridge. Original work published 1656.

Bogardus, E. S. 1927. "Leadership and Social Distance." *Sociology and Social Research* 12:173–178.

Bogardus, E. S. 1928. "World Leadership Types." *Sociology and Social Research* 12:573–599.

Bogardus, E. S. 1929. "Leadership and Attitudes." *Sociology and Social Research* 13:377–381.

Bogardus, E. S. 1934. *Leaders and Leadership*. New York: Appleton-Century-Crofts, Inc.

Boone, T. A. 1977. "A Practical Leadership Paradigm." In J. E. Jones and J. W. Pfeiffer, eds., *The 1977 Annual Handbook for Group Facilitators*, 110–114. San Diego: University Associates.

Bowers, D. G., and Seashore, S. E. 1966. "Predicting Organizational Effectiveness with a Four-Factor Theory of Leadership." *Administrative Science Quarterly* 11, no. 2: 238–263.

Braddy, P. W.; Gooty, J.; Fleenor, J. W.; and Yammarino, F. J. 2014. "Leader Behaviors and Career Derailment Potential: A Multi-analytic Method Examination of Rating Source and Self-Other Agreement." *Leadership Quarterly* 25, no. 2: 373–390.

Bradley, T. P.; Allen, J. M.; Hamilton, S.; and Filgo, S. K. 2006. "Leadership Perception: Analysis of 360-Degree Feedback." *Performance Improvement Quarterly* 19, no.1: 7–23.

Bratton, J.; Grint, K.; and Nelson, D. L. 2005. *Organizational Leadership*. Mason, OH: South-Western.

Brewer, A. 2014. *Leadership, Coaching and Followership: An Important Equation*. Dordrecht: Springer.

Bromley, D. B. 1993. *Reputation, Image and Impression Management*. Chichester: John Wiley and Sons.

Brown, B. 2018. *Dare to Lead*. New York: Random House.

Buckingham, M., and Coffman, C. 1999. *First, Break All the Rules: What the World's Greatest Managers Do Differently*. New York: Simon and Schuster.

Bundel, C. M. 1930. "Is Leadership Losing Its Importance?" *Infantry Journal* 36, no. 4: 339–349.

Burns, J. M. 1976. *Edward Kennedy and the Camelot legacy*. New York: W. W. Norton.

Burns, J. M. 1979. *Leadership*. New York: Harper and Row. Original work published 1978.

Burns, J. M. 1998. "Foreword." In J. B. Ciulla, ed., *Ethics: The Heart of Leadership*, ix–xii. Westport, CT: Quorum.

Cable, D. M., and Yu, K. Y T. 2006. "Managing Job Seeker's Organizational Image Beliefs: The Role of Media Richness and Media Credibility." *Journal of Applied Psychology* 91, no. 4: 828–840.

Calder, B. J. 1977. "An Attribution Theory of Leadership." In B. M. Staw and G. R. Salancik, eds., *New Directions in Organizational Behavior*, 179–204. Chicago: St. Clair.

Campbell, D. P. 1992. "The Leadership Characteristics of Leadership Researchers." In K. E. Clark, M. B. Clark, and D. P. Campbell, eds., *Impact of Leadership*, 25–36. Greensboro, NC: Center for Creative Leadership.

Caraley, D. J. 2009. "Three Trends over Eight Presidential Elections, 1980–2008: Toward the Emergence of a Democratic Majority Realignment?" *Political Science Quarterly* 124, no. 3: 423–442.

Carsten, M. K.; Harmes, P.; and Uhl-Bien, M. 2014. "Exploring Historical Perspectives of Followership: The Need for an Expanded View of Followers and the Follower Role." In L. M. Lapierre and M. K. Carsten, eds., *Followership: What Is It and Why Do People Follow?*, 4–25. Bingley: Emerald.

Carsten, M. K., and Uhl-Bien, M. 2012. "Follower Beliefs in the Co-Production of Leadership: Examining Upward Communication and the Moderating Role of Context." *Zeitschrift für Psychologie* 220, no. 4: 210–220.

Carter, L. F. 1953. "Leadership and Small-Group Behavior." In M. Sherif and M. O. Wilson, eds., *Group Relations at the Crossroads*, 257–281. New York: Harper and Brothers.

Cawdrey, R. 1604. *A Table Alphabeticall*. Printed by I. R. for Edmund Weaner.

Chapin, F. S. 1924. "Leadership and Group Activity." *Journal of Applied Psychology* 8, no. 1: 141–145.

Chemers, M. M. 1997. *An Integrative Theory of Leadership*. Mahwah, NJ: Lawrence Erlbaum Associates.

Chemers, M. M. 2000. "Leadership Research and Theory: A Functional Integration." *Group Dynamics: Theory, Research, and Practice* 4, no. 1: 27–43.

Chemers, M. M. 2001. "Leadership Effectiveness: An Integrative Review." In M. A. Hogg and R. S. Tindale, eds., *Blackwell Handbook of Social Psychology: Group Processes*. 376–399. Oxford: Blackwell.

Chen, G.; Sharma, P. N.; Edinger, S. K.; Shapiro, D. L.; and Farh, J.-L. 2011. Motivating and Demotivating Forces in Teams: Cross-Level Influences of Empowering Leadership and Relationship Conflict. *Journal of Applied Psychology* 96, no. 3: 541–557.

Childers, T. 1984. "Who, Indeed, Did Vote for Hitler?" *Central European History* 17, no. 1: 45–53.

Chrobot-Mason, D. 2014. "Leadership in a Diverse Workplace." In D. V. Day, ed., *The Oxford Handbook of Leadership and Organization*, 683–708. New York: Oxford University Press.

Ciulla, J. B. 2002. "Trust and the Future of Leadership." In N. E. Bowie, ed., *The Blackwell Guide to Business Ethics*, 334–351. Oxford: Blackwell.

Ciulla, J. B. 2018. "Ethics and Effectiveness: The Nature of Good Leadership. In J. Antonakis and D. V. Day, eds., *The Nature of Leadership*, 3rd ed., 438–468. Thousand Oaks, CA: SAGE.

Clark, K. E., and Clark, M. B. 1994. *Choosing to Lead*. Greensboro, NC: Leadership.

Clark, M. B.; Freeman, F. H.; and Gregory, R. A., eds. 1986. *Leadership Education: A Source Book*. Greensboro, NC: Center for Creative Leadership.

Cockeram, H. 1930. *The English Dictionarie of 1623 by Henry Cockeram*. New York: Huntington Press. Original work published 1623.

Coles, E. 1971. *An English Dictionary, 1676*. Menston, England: Scholar Press. Original work published 1676.

Cook, A. S.; Zill, A.; and Meyer, B. 2020. Observing Leadership as Behavior in Teams and Herds—An Ethological Approach to Shared Leadership Research. *The Leadership Quarterly* 31, no. 2: 1–14. https://doi-org.ezproxy.neu.edu/10.1016/j.leaqua.2019.05.003.

Cooley, C. H. 1902. *Human Nature and the Social Order*. New York: Charles Scribner's Sons.

Cooley, C. H. 1909. *Social Organization: A Study of the Larger Mind*. New York: Charles Scribner's Sons.

Cooper, J. B., and McGaugh, J. L. 1963. *Integrating Principles of Social psychology*. Cambridge, MA: Schenkman.

Copeland, N. 1942. *Psychology and the Soldier*. Harrisburg, PA: Military Service.

Costello, R. B. 1992. *Random House Webster's College Dictionary*. New York: Random House. Original work published 1991.

Cote, R. 2017. "A Comparison of Leadership Theories in an Organizational Environment." *International Journal of Business Administration* 8, no. 5: 28–35. http://www.sciedu.ca/journal/index.php/ijba/article/view/11836/7283.

Cowie, A. P. ed. 2009. *The Oxford History of English Lexicography, Volume I: General Purpose Dictionaries.* New York: Oxford University Press.

Cowley, W. H. 1928. "Three Distinctions in the Study of Leaders." *Journal of Abnormal and Social Psychology* 23, no. 2: 144–157.

Cowley, W. H. 1931. "The Traits of Face-to-Face Leaders." *Journal of Abnormal and Social Psychology* 26, no. 3: 304–313.

Cribbin, J. J. 1981. *Leadership: Strategies for Organizational Effectiveness.* New York: AMACOM.

Cronin, T. E. 1980. *The State of the Presidency*, 2nd ed. Boston: Little, Brown.

Crossman, B., and Crossman, J. 2011. "Conceptualising Followership—A Review of the Literature." *Leadership* 7, no. 4: 481–497.

Cullen, J. 2015. "Leading through Contingencies." In B. Carroll, J. Ford, and S. Taylor, eds., *Leadership: Contemporary Critical Perspectives*, 45–68. Los Angeles: SAGE.

Dachler, H. P. 1984. "Chapter 5 Commentary: On Refocusing Leadership from a Social Systems Perspective of Management." In J. G. Hunt, D. M. Hosking, C. A. Schriesheim, and R. Stewart, eds., *Leaders and Managers: International Perspectives on Managerial Behavior and Leadership*, 100–108. Elmsford, NY: Pergamon.

Daft, R. L. 2002. *The Leadership Experience*, 2nd ed. Mason, OH: Thompson Southwestern.

Daft, R. L. 2008. *Management*, 8th ed. Mason, OH: South-Western Cengage Learning.

Daft, R. L. 2018. *Management*, 13th ed. Boston: Cengage Learning.

Dansereau, F.; Graen, G.; and Haga, W. J. 1975. "A Vertical Dyad Linkage Approach to Leadership in Formal Organizations." *Organizational Behavior and Human Performance* 13:46–78.

Dansereau, F.; Yammarino, F. J.; Markham, S. E.; Alutto, J. A.; Newman, J.; Dumas, M.; Nachman, S. A.; Naughton, T. J.; Kim, K.; Al-Kelabi, S. A.; Lee, S.; and Keller, T. 1995. "Individualized Leadership: A New Multi-level Approach." *Leadership Quarterly* 6, no. 3: 413–450.

Dasborough, M. T., and Ashkanasy, N. M. 2002. "Emotion and Attribution of Intentionality in Leader-Member Relationships." *Leadership Quarterly* 13, no. 5: 615–634.

Davies, P., ed. 1982. *The American Heritage Dictionary: Second College Edition*. Boston: Houghton Mifflin.

Davis, K. 1962. *Human Relations at Work*, 2nd ed. New York: McGraw Hill.

Davis, K., and Newstrom, J. W. 1985. *Human Behavior at Work: Organizational Behavior*, 2nd ed. New York: McGraw Hill.

Day, D. V. 2000. "Leadership Development: A Review of Context." *Leadership Quarterly* 11, no. 4: 581–613.

Day, D. V. 2004. "Leadership Development." In G. R. Goethals, G. J. Sorenson, and J. M. Burns, eds., *Encyclopedia of Leadership*, 2:840–844. Thousand Oaks, CA: SAGE.

Day, D. V. 2014a. "Introduction: Leadership and Organizations." In D. V. Day, ed., *The Oxford Handbook of Leadership and Organization*, 3–12. New York: Oxford University Press.

Day, D. V. 2014b. "The Future of Leadership: Challenges and Prospects." In D. V. Day, ed., *The Oxford Handbook of Leadership and Organization*, 859–868. New York: Oxford University Press.

Day, D. V., and Antonakis, J. 2012. "Leadership: Past, Present, and Future." In D. V. Day and J. Antonakis, eds., *The Nature of Leadership*, 2nd ed., 3–25. Thousand Oaks, CA: SAGE.

Day, D. V.; Fleenor, J. W.; Atwater, L. E.; Sturm, R. E.; and McKee, R. A. 2014. "Advances in Leader and Leadership Development: A Review of 25 Years of Research and Theory." *Leadership Quarterly* 25, no. 1: 63–82.

Deal, T. E., and Kennedy, A. A. 1982. *Corporate Cultures: The Rites and Rituals of Corporate Life*. Reading, MA: Addison-Wesley.

de Haan, E. 2016. "The Leadership Shadow: How to Recognise and Avoid Derailment, Hubris and Overdrive." *Leadership* 12, no. 4: 504–512.

Dede, N. P., and Ayranci, E. 2014. "Effects of Motivation to Lead on Leadership Preference: An Empirical Study." *International Journal of Academic Research in Business Research and Social Sciences* 4, no. 7: 241–270.

Den Hartog, D. N., and Dickson, M. W. 2012. "Leadership and Culture." In D. V. Day and J. Antonakis, eds., *The Nature of Leadership*, 2nd ed., 393–436. Thousand Oaks, CA: SAGE.

Den Hartog, D. N., and Dickson, M. W. 2018. "Leadership, Culture, and Globalization." In J. Antonakis and D. V. Day, eds., *The Nature of Leadership*, 3rd ed., 327–353. Thousand Oaks, CA: SAGE.

Department of the Army United States of America. 2019. *ADP 6-22 Army Leadership and the Profession*. Retrieved January 27, 2022. https://armypubs.army.mil/epubs/DR_pubs/DR_a/pdf/web/ARN20039_ADP%206-22%20C1%20FINAL%20WEB.pdf.

DeRue, D. S., and Myers, C. G. 2014. "Leadership Development: A Review and Agenda for Future Research." In D. V. Day, ed., *The Oxford Handbook of Leadership and Organization*, 832–856. New York: Oxford University Press.

Dessler, G. 2001. *Management: Leading People and Organizations in the 21st Century*. Upper Saddle River, NJ: Prentice Hall.

DeVille, J. 1984. *The Psychology of Leadership: Managing Resources and Relationships*. New York: Mentor.

Dinh, J. E.; Lord, R. G.; Gardner, W. L.; Meuser, J. D.; Liden, R. C.; and Hu, J. 2014. "Leadership Theory and Research in the New Millennium: Current Theoretical Trends and Changing Perspectives." *Leadership Quarterly* 25, no. 1: 36–62.

Downton, J. V. 1973. *Rebel leadership: Commitment and Charisma in a Revolutionary Process*. New York: Free.

Drath, W. H.; McCauley, C. D.; Van Velsor, C. J.; O'Connor, P. M. G.; and McGuire, J. B. 2008. "Direction, Alignment, Commitment: Toward a More Integrative Ontology of Leadership. *Leadership Quarterly* 19, no. 6: 635–653.

Drath, W. H., and Palus, C. J. 1994. *Making Common Sense: Leadership as Meaning-Making in a Community of Practice*. Greensboro, NC: Center for Creative Leadership.

Drucker, P. F. 1954. *The Practice of Management*. New York: Harper and Row.

Drucker, P. F. 1967. *The Effective Executive*. New York: Harper and Row.

Drucker, P. F. 1988. "Drucker on Management: Leadership: More Doing than Dash." *Wall Street Journal*, January 6. https://link.ezproxy.neu.edu/login?url=https://www-proquest-com.ezproxy.neu.edu/newspapers/drucker-on-managemen t-leadership-more-doing-than/docview/398022047/se-2?accountid=12826.

DuBrin, A. J. 2001. *Leadership: Research Findings, Practice, and Skills*, 3rd ed. Boston: Houghton Mifflin.

Dulebohn, J. H.; Bommer, W. H.; Liden, R. C.; Brouer, R. L.; and Ferris, G. R. 2012. A Meta-analysis of Antecedents and Consequences of Leader-Member Exchange: Integrating the Past with an Eye toward the Future." *Journal of Management* 38, no. 6: 1715–1759. DOI:10.1177/0149206311415280.

Dupuy, R. E., and Dupuy, T. N. 1959. *Brave Men and Great Captains.* New York: Harper and Brothers.

Eacott, S. 2013. "'Leadership' and the Social: Time, Space and the Epistemic." *International Journal of Educational Management* 27, no. 1: 91–101.

Eagly, A. H., and Carli, L. L. 2007. *Through the Labyrinth: The Truth about How Women Become Leaders.* Boston: Harvard Business School Press.

Emery, H. G., and Brewster, K. G. 1927. *The New Century Dictionary of the English Language*, Vol. 1. New York: Century.

England, G. W.; Dhingra, O. P.; and Agarwal, N. C. 1974. *The Manager and the Man: A Cross-cultural Study of Personal Values.* Kent, OH: Comparative Administration Research Institute of the Center for Business and Economic Research, Kent State University Press.

Epitropaki, O.; Martin, R.; and Thomas, G. 2018. "Relationship Leadership." In J. Antonakis and D. V. Day, eds., *The Mature of Leadership.* 3rd ed., 109–137. Thousand Oaks, CA: SAGE.

Etzioni, A. 1965. "Dual Leadership in Complex Organizations." *American Sociological Review* 30, no. 5: 688–698.

Evans, M. G. 1970. "The Effects of Supervisory Behavior on the Path-Goal Relationship." *Organizational Behavior and Human Performance* 5, no. 3: 277–298.

Evans, M. G. 1996. "R. J. House's 'A Path-Goal Theory of Leader Effectiveness.'" *Leadership Quarterly* 7, no. 3: 305–309.

Fairhurst, G. T., and Grant, D. 2010. "The Social Construction of Leadership: A Sailing Guide." *Management Communication Quarterly* 24, no. 2: 171–210.

Ferguson, T., and Voth, H.-J. 2008. "Betting on Hitler: The Value of Political Connections in Nazi Germany." *Quarterly Journal of Economics* 123, no. 1: 101–137.

Fiedler, F. E. 1965. "Engineer the Job to Fit the Manager." *Harvard Business Review* 43, no. 5: 115–122.

Fiedler, F. E. 1967. *A Theory of Leadership Effectiveness*. New York: McGraw Hill.

Fischer, T., Dietz, J., and Antonakis, J. 2017. "Leadership Process Models: A Review and Synthesis." *Journal of Management* 43, no. 6: 1726–1753.

Fiske, S. T., and Berdahl, J. 2007. "Social Power." In A. W. Kruglanski and E. Tory Higgins, eds., *Social Psychology: Handbook of Basic Principles*, 2nd ed., 678–692. New York: Guilford.

Fitzsimmons, T. W., and Callan, V. J. 2020. "The Diversity Gap in Leadership: What Are We Missing in Current Theorizing?" *Leadership Quarterly* 31, no. 4: 1–13. https://www.sciencedirect.com/science/article/pii/S1048984318307513.

Fleishman, E. A. 1973. "Twenty Years of Consideration and Structure." In E. A. Fleishman and J. G. Hunt, eds., *Current Developments in the Study of Leadership: A Centennial Event Symposium Held at Southern Illinois University at Carbondale.* Carbondale: Southern Illinois University Press.

Fleishman, E. A.; Mumford, M. D.; Zaccaro, S. J.; Levin, K. Y.; Korotkin, A. L.; and Hein, M. B. 1991. "Taxonomic Efforts in the Description of Leader Behavior: A Synthesis and Functional Interpretation." *Leadership Quarterly* 2, no. 4: 245–287.

Fleishman, E. A., and Peters, D. R. 1962. "Interpersonal Values, Leadership Attitudes and Managerial Success." *Personnel Psychology* 15, no. 2: 127–143.

Flexner, S. B. 1987. *The Random House Dictionary of the English Language*, 2nd ed. New York: Random House.

Follett, M. P. 1933. "The Essentials of Leadership." In L. Urwick, ed., *Freedom and Co-ordination: Lectures in Business Organization*, 47–60. New York: Garland. Original work published 1949.

Freeman, F. H.; Knott, K. B.; and Schwartz, M. K. 1994. "Courses and Programs." In F. H. Freeman, K. B. Knott, and M. K. Schwartz, eds., *Leadership Education 1994–1995: A Source Book*. Greensboro, NC: Center for Creative Leadership.

French, J. R., Jr. 1956. "A Formal Theory of Social Power." *Psychological Review* 63, no. 3: 181–194.

Friedrich, C. J. 1961. "Political Leadership and the Problem of Charismatic Power." *Journal of Politics* 23, no. 1: 3–24.

Friend, J. H., and Guralnik, D. B., eds. 1951. *Webster's New World Dictionary of the American Language Encyclopedic Edition.* Cleveland: World.

Friend, J. H., and Guralnik, D. B., eds. 1953. *Webster's New World Dictionary of the American Language College Edition.* Cleveland: World.

Funk, I. K. 1893. *A Standard Dictionary of the English Language,* Vol. 1. New York: Funk and Wagnalls.

Galinsky, A. D.; Jordan, J.; and Sivanathan, N. 2008. "Harnessing Power to Capture Leadership." In J. B. Ciulla, C. Hoyt, G. R. Goethals, and D. R. Forsyth, eds., *Leadership at the Crossroads,* 1:283–299. Westport, CT: Praeger.

Gardner, J. W. 1986. *The Nature of Leadership: Introductory Considerations.* Washington, DC: Independent Sector.

Gardner, J. W. 1988. *Leadership: An Overview.* Washington, DC: Independent Sector.

Gardner, W. L.; Lowe, K. B.; Mcuser, J. D.; Noghani, F.; Gullifor, D. P.; and Cogliser, C. C. 2020. "The Leadership Trilogy: A Review of the Third Decade of *The Leadership Quarterly.*" *Leadership Quarterly* 31, no. 1: 1–26. https://doi-org.ezproxy.neu.edu/10.1016/j.leaqua.2019.101379.

Gardner, W. L.; Lowe, K. B.; Moss, T. W.; Mahoney, K. T.; and Cogliser, C. C. 2010. "Scholarly Leadership of the Study of Leadership: A Review of *The Leadership Quarterly's* Second Decade, 2000–2009." *Leadership Quarterly* 21, no. 6: 922–958.

Garretsen, H.; Stoker, J. I.; and Weber, R. A. 2020. "Economic Perspectives on Leadership: Concepts, Causality, and Context in Leadership Research." *Leadership Quarterly* 31, no. 3: 9–11.

Gazophylacium Anglicanum. 1969. Menston, England: Scholar. Original work published 1689.

Georgopoulos, G. S.; Mahoney, G. M.; and Jones, N. W., Jr. 1957. "A Path-Goal Approach to Productivity." *Journal of Applied Psychology* 41, no. 6: 345–353.

Gibb, C. A. 1947. "The Principles and Traits of Leadership." *Journal of Abnormal Psychology* 42, no. 3: 267–284.

Gibb, C. A. 1954. "Leadership." In G. Lindzey, ed., *Handbook of Social Psychology*, 2:877–920. Reading, MA: Addison-Wesley.

Gibb, C. A. 1958. "An Interactional View of the Emergence of Leadership." *Australian Journal of Psychology* 10, no. 1: 101–110.

Gibb, C. A. 1969. "Leadership." In G. Lindzey and R. Aronson, eds., *Handbook of Social Psychology*, 2nd ed., 4:205–282. Reading, MA: Addison-Wesley.

Gini, A. 1997. "Moral Leadership: An Overview." *Journal of Business Ethics* 16, no. 3: 323–330.

Goeschel, C. 2017. "Biography, Political Leadership, and Foreign Policy Reconsidered: The Cases of Mussolini and Hitler." *European Review of International Studies* 4, no. 2 + 3: 5–19.

Goffee, R., and Jones, G. 2001. "Followership—It's Personal, Too." *Harvard Business Review* 79, no. 11: 148.

Gove, P. B., ed. 1961. *Webster's Third New International Dictionary of the English Language Unabridged*, 3rd ed. Springfield, MA: G. and C. Merriam.

Gove, P. B., ed. 1963. *Webster's Seventh New Collegiate Dictionary*, 7th ed. Springfield, MA: G. and C. Merriam.

Graen, G., and Cashman, J. 1975. "A Role-Making Model of Leadership in Formal Organizations: A Developmental Approach." In J. G. Hunt and L. L. Larson, eds., *Leadership Frontiers*, 143–166. Kent, OH: Kent State University Press.

Graen, G.; Novak, M. A.; and Sommerkamp, P. 1982. "The Effects of Leader—Member Exchange and Job Design on Productivity and Satisfaction: Testing a Dual Attachment Model." *Organizational Behavior and Human Performance* 30, no. 1: 109–131.

Graen, G.; Rowold, J.; and Heinitz, K. 2010. "Issues in Operationalizing and Comparing Leadership Constructs." *Leadership Quarterly* 21, no. 3: 563–575.

Graen, G. B., and Uhl-Bien, M. 1991. "The Transformation of Professionals into Self-Managing and Partially Self-Designing Contributors: Toward a Theory of Leadership-Making." *Journal of Management Systems* 3, no. 3: 25–39.

Graen, G. B., and Uhl-Bien, M. 1995. "Relationship-Based Approach to Leadership: Development of Leader-Member Exchange (LMX) Theory of Leadership over 25 Years: Applying a Multi-level Multi-domain Perspective." *Leadership Quarterly* 6, no. 2: 219–247.

Green, J. 1996. *Chasing the Sun: Dictionary Makers and the Dictionaries They Made*. New York: Henry Holt.

Greenleaf, R. K. 1972. *The Institution as Servant*. Cambridge, MA: Center for Applied Studies.

Greenleaf, R. K. 1973. *The Servant as Leader*, rev. ed. Westfield, IN: Greenleaf Center for Servant Leadership.

Greenleaf, R. K. 1977. *Servant Leadership: A Journey into the Nature of Legitimate Power and Greatness*. Mahwah, NJ: Paulist.

Grint, K. 2000. *The Arts of Leadership*. New York: Oxford University Press.

Grint, K. 2005. *Leadership: Limits and Possibilities*. Basingstoke: Palgrave Macmillan.

Grint, K. 2010a. *Leadership: A Very Short Introduction*. New York: Oxford University Press.

Grint, K. 2010b. "The Cuckoo Clock Syndrome: Addicted to Command, Allergic to Leadership." *European Management Journal* 28, no. 4: 306–313.

Grint, K.; Smolovic Jones, O.; and Holt, C. 2016. "What Is Leadership: Person, Result, Position or Process, or All or None of These?" In J. Storey, J. Hartley, J.-L. Denis, P. 't Hart, and D. Ulrich, eds., *Leadership Studies: The Routledge Companion to Leadership*, 3–20. London: Routledge.

Gronn, P. 1996. "From Transactions to Transformations: A New World Order in the Study of Leadership?" *Educational Management and Administration* 24, no. 1: 7–30. https://journals.sagepub.com/doi/10.1177/0263211X96241002.

Gronn, P. 1997. "Leading for Learning: Organizational Transformation and the Formation of Leaders." *Journal of Management Development* 16, no. 4: 274–283.

Gronn, P. 2002. "Distributed Leadership as a Unit of Analysis." *Leadership Quarterly* 13, no. 4: 423–451.

Guralnik, D. B., ed. 1970. *Webster's New World Dictionary of the American Language, Second College Edition*. Cleveland: World Publishing Company.

Guthrie, K. L.; Batchelder, J. M.; and Hu, P. 2019. *Examining Degree Types of Academic Leadership Programs in the United States*. Tallahassee, FL: Leadership Learning Research Center, Florida State University.

Hackman, M. Z., and Johnson, C. E. 2013. *Leadership: A Communication Perspective*, 6th ed. Long Grove, IL: Waveland.

Haimann, T., and Hilgert, R. L. 1977. *Supervision: Concepts and Practices of Management*, 2nd ed. Cincinnati: South-Western.

Halpin, S. M. 2011. "Historical Influence on the Changing Nature of leadership within the Military Environment." *Military Psychology* 23, no. 5: 479–488.

Hamilton, R. F. 1986. "Hitler's Electoral Support: Recent Findings and Theoretical Implications." *Canadian Journal of Sociology* 11, no. 1: 1–34.

Hamstra, M.; Van Yperen, N.; Wisse, B.; and Sassenberg, K. 2014. "Transformational and Transactional Leadership and Followers' Achievement Goals." *Journal of Business and Psychology* 29, no. 3: .413–425.

Harvey, M. 2011. "Questioning Leadership: An Integrative Model." In M. Harvey and R. E. Riggio, eds., *Leadership Studies: The Dialogue of Disciplines*, 199–229. Cheltenham: Edward Elgar.

Heifetz, R. 1988. Leadership Expert Ronald Heifetz." *Inc.* 10, no. 10: 36–48.

Heifetz, R. A. 1994. *Leadership without Easy Answers*. Cambridge, MA: Belknap.

Heifetz, R. A. 2007. "The Scholarly/Practical Challenge of Leadership." In R. A. Cuoto, ed., *Reflections on Leadership*, 31–55. Lanham, MD: University Press of America.

Heifetz, R. A., and Sinder, R. M. 1988. "Political Leadership: Managing the Public's Problem Solving." In R. B. Reich, ed., *The Power of Public Ideas*, 179–203. Cambridge, MA: Ballinger.

Helmick, E. A. 1924. "In US Army Command and General Staff College." In *Psychology and Leadership: Eight Lectures, on Selected Phases of These Subjects, Delivered at the General Service Schools*, 2nd ed, 149–170. Fort Leavenworth, KS: General Service Schools.

Hemphill, J. K. 1949a. *Situational Factors in Leadership*. Columbus, OH: Bureau of Educational Research, Ohio State University.

Hemphill, J. K. 1949b. "The Leader and His Group." *Educational Research Bulletin* 28, no. 9: 225–229, 245–246.

Hemphill, J. K. 1961. "Why People Attempt to Lead." In L. Petrullo and B. M. Bass, eds., *Leadership and Interpersonal Behavior*, 201–215. New York: Holt, Reinhart, and Winston.

Hemphill, J. K., and Coons, A. E. 1957. "Development of the Leader Behavior Description Questionnaire." In R. M. Stogdill and A. E. Coons, eds., *Leader Behavior: Its Description and Measurement*, 6–38. Columbus, OH: Bureau of Business Research, Ohio State University.

Hersey, P., and Blanchard, K. H. 1972. *Management of Organizational Behavior: Utilizing Human Resources*, 2nd ed. Englewood Cliffs, NJ: Prentice Hall.

Hersey, P., and Blanchard, K. H. 1974. "So You Want to Know Your Leadership Style? Measuring How You Behave in a Situational Leadership Framework." *Training and Development Journal* 28, no. 2: 22–37.

Hersey, P., and Blanchard, K. H. 1988. *Management of Organizational Behavior: Utilizing Human Resources*, 5th ed. Englewood Cliffs, NJ: Prentice Hall.

Hersey, P.; Blanchard, K. H.; and Johnson, D. E. 2001. *Management of Organizational Behavior: Leading Human Resources*, 8th ed. Upper Saddle River, NJ: Pearson.

Hersey, P.; Blanchard, K. H.; and Johnson, D. E. 2008. *Management of Organizational Behavior: Leading Human Resources*, 9th ed. Upper Saddle River, NJ: Pearson.

Hersey, P.; Blanchard, K. H.; and Johnson, D. E. 2013. *Management of Organizational Behavior: Leading Human Resources*, 10th ed. Upper Saddle River, NJ: Pearson.

Hersey, P., Blanchard, K. H., and Natemeyer, W. E. 1979. "Situational Leadership, Perception, and the Impact of Power." *Group and Organization Studies* 4, no. 4: 418–428.

Hesselbein, F. 2002. *Hesselbein on Leadership*. San Francisco: Jossey-Bass.

Hitler, A. 1939. *Mein Kampf*. J. Murphy, trans. London: Hurst and Blackett. Original work published 1925.

Hogan, R.; Curphy, G. J.; and Hogan, J. 1994. "What We Know about Leadership: Effectiveness and Personality." *American Psychologist* 49, no. 6: 493–504.

Hogan, R., and Kaiser, R. B. 2005. "What We Know about Leadership." *Review of General Psychology* 9, no. 2: 169–180.

Hogg, M. A. 2001. "What We Know about Leadership." *Personality and Social Psychology Review* 5, no. 3: 184–200.

Hogg, M. A. 2008. "Social Identity Theory of Leadership." In J. B. Ciulla, C. Hoyt, G. R. Goethals, and D. R. Forsyth, eds., *Leadership at the Crossroads*, 1:62–77. Westport, CT: Praeger.

Hogg, M. A. 2013. "Leadership." In J. M. Levine, ed., *Group Processes*, 241–266. New York: Psychology.

Hogg, M. A.; Martin, R.; and Weeden, K. 2003. "Leader-Member Relations and Social Identity." In D. van Knippenberg and M. A. Hogg, eds., *Leadership and Power: Identity Processes in Groups and Organizations*, 18–33. London: SAGE.

Hollander, E. P. 1964. *Leaders, Groups, and Influence*. New York: Oxford University Press.

Hollander, E. P. 1978. *Leadership Dynamics*. New York: Free.

Hollander, E. P. 1986. "On the Central Role of Leadership Processes." *Applied Psychology* 35, no. 1: 39–52.

Hollander, E. P., and Julian, J. W. 1968. "Leadership." In E. F. Borgatta and W. W. Lambert, eds., *Handbook of Personality Theory and Research*, 890–899. Chicago: Rand McNally.

Hollander, E. P., and Julian, J. W. 1969. "Contemporary Trends in the Analysis of Leadership Processes." *Psychological Bulletin*, no. 5: 387–397.

Hollander, E. P., and Offermann, L. R. 1990. "Power and Leadership in Organizations: Relationships in Transition." *American Psychologist* 45, no. 1: 179–189.

Kleinedler, S. R. 2020. "The American Heritage Dictionary of the English Language." https://ahdictionary.com/word/search. html?q=leadership.

House, R. J. 1971. "A Path Goal Theory of Leader Effectiveness." *Administrative Science Quarterly* 16, no. 3: 321–338.

House, R. J. 1995. "Leadership in the Twenty-First Century: A Speculative Inquiry." In A. Howard, ed., *The Changing Nature of Work*, 411–450. San Francisco: Jossey-Bass.

House, R. J. 1996. "Path-Goal Theory of Leadership: Lessons, Legacy, and a Reformulated Theory." *Leadership Quarterly* 7, no. 3: 323–352.

House, R.; Javidan, M.; Hanges, P.; and Dorfman, P. 2002. "Understanding Cultures and Implicit Leadership Theories across the Globe: An Introduction to GLOBE Project." *Journal of World Business* 37, no. 1: 3–10.

House, R. J.; Javidan, M.; Hanges, P. J.; Dorfman, P. W.; and Gupta, V., eds. 2004. *Culture, Leadership, and Organizations: The GLOBE Study of 62 Societies*. Thousand Oaks, CA: SAGE.

House, R. J., and Mitchell, R. R. 1974. "Path-Goal Theory of Leadership." *Journal of Contemporary Business* 3:81–97.

Howell, J. M. 1988. "Two Faces of Charisma: Socialized and Personalized Leadership in Organizations." In J. A. Conger and R. N. Kanungo, eds., *Charismatic Leadership: The Elusive Factor in Organizational Effectiveness*, 213–236. San Francisco: Jossey-Bass.

Howell, J. M., and Avolio, B. J. 1992. "The Ethics of Charismatic Leadership: Submission or Liberation?" *Academy of Management Executive* 6, no. 2: 43–54.

Hughbank, R. J., and Horn, L. C. 2013. "Traits and Behavior: Psychological Approaches to Leadership." In A. H. Normore and N. Erbe, eds., *Collective Efficacy: Psychological Approaches to Leadership*, 20:245–260. Bingley: Emerald Group.

Hughes, R. L.; Ginnett, R. C.; and Curphy, G. J. 1993. *Leadership: Enhancing the Lessons of Experience*. Homewood, IL: Irwin.

Hughes, R. L.; Ginnett, R. C.; and Curphy, G. J. 2009. *Leadership: Enhancing the Lessons of Experience*, 6th ed. Homewood, IL: Irwin.

Hughes, R. L.; Ginnett, R. C.; and Curphy, G. J. 2018. *Leadership: Enhancing the Lessons of Experience*, 9th ed. Homewood, IL: Irwin.

Hunt, J. B. 2000. "Travel Experience in the Formation of Leadership: John Quincy Adams, Frederick Douglass, and Jane Addams." *Journal of Leadership and Organizational Studies* 7, no. 1: 92–106.

Hurley, P. J., and Watson, L. 2018. *A Concise Introduction to Logic*, 13th ed. Boston: Cengage Learning.

Ikenberry, G. J. 1996. "The Future of International Leadership." *Political Science Quarterly* 111, no. 3: 385–402.

International Leadership Association. 2008. "Leadership Legacy Program: Joseph C. Rost 2008 Lifetime Achievement Award Winner." Retrieved May 13, 2021. http://www.ila-net.org/LeadershipLegacy/Joseph_Rost.html.

Jacobs, T. O. 1970. *Leadership and Exchange in Social Situations*. Alexandria, VA: Human Resources Research Organization.

Jacobs, T. O., and Jaques, E. 1990. "Military Executive Leadership." In K. E. Clark and M. B. Clark, eds., *Measures of Leadership*, 281–295: West Orange, NJ: Leadership Library of America.

Jago, A. G. 1982. "Leadership: Perspectives in Theory and Research." *Management Science* 28, no. 3: 315–336.

Janda, K. F. 1960. "Towards the Explication of the Concept of Leadership in Terms of the Concept of Power." *Human Relations* 13, no. 4: 345–363.

Jennings, H. H. 1944. "Leadership—A Dynamic Redefinition." *Journal of Educational Psychology* 17, no. 7: 431–433.

Jennings, H. H. 1947. "Leadership and Sociometric Choice." *Sociometry* 10, no. 1: 32–49.

Jewell, E. J., and Abate, F., eds. 2001. *The New Oxford American Dictionary*. Oxford: Oxford University Press.

Johnson, S. 1755. *A Dictionary of the English Language*. Printed by W. Strahan.

Jones, G. R., and George, J. M. 2007. *Essentials of Contemporary Management*, 2nd ed.. Boston: McGraw Hill.

Jones, J. M. 2021. "Last Trump Job Approval 34%; Average is Record-Low 41%." Gallup. Accessed January 18, 2021. https://news.gallup.com/poll/328637/last-trump-job-approval-average-record-low.aspx.

Kan, M. M., and Parry, K. W. 2004. "Identifying Paradox: A Grounded Theory of Leadership in Overcoming Resistance to Change." *Leadership Quarterly* 15, no. 4: 467–491.

Katz, D., and Kahn, R. L. 1966. *The Social Psychology of Organizations.* New York: John Wiley and Sons.

Kelemen, T. K.; Matthews, S. H.; and Breevaart, K. 2020. "Leading Day-to-Day: A Review of the Daily Causes and Consequences of Leadership Behaviors." *Leadership Quarterly* 31, no. 1. https://doi.org/10.1016/j.leaqua.2019.101344.

Kellerman, B. 2008. *Followership: How Followers Are Creating Change and Changing Leaders.* Boston: Harvard Business Press.

Kellerman, B. 2019. "The Future of Followership." *Strategy and Leadership* 47, no. 5: 42–46.

Kellerman, B., and Webster, S. W. 2001. "The Recent Literature on Public Leadership: Reviewed and Considered." *Leadership Quarterly* 12, no. 4: 485–514.

Kersey, J. 1713. *A New English Dictionary*, 2nd ed. Printed for Robert Knaplock and R. and J. Bonwicke.

Kilburg, R. R., and Donohue, M. D. 2011. "Toward a 'Grand Unifying Theory' of Leadership: Implications for Consulting Psychology." *Consulting Psychology Journal: Practice and Research* 63, no. 1: 6–25.

Kim, M., and Beehr, T. A. 2020. "Empowering Leadership: Leading People to Be Present through Affective Organizational Commitment?" *International Journal of Human Resource Management* 31, no. 16: 2017–2044.

Kim, W., and Mauborgne, R. 1992. "Parables of Leadership." *Harvard Business Review* 74, no. 2: 123–128.

King, A. S. 1990. "Evolution of Leadership Theory." *Vikalpa: The Journal for Decision Makers* 15, no. 2: 43–56.

King, G.; Rosen, O.; Tanner, M.; and Wagner, A. F. 2008. "Ordinary Economic Voting Behavior in the Extraordinary Election of Adolph Hitler." *Journal of Economic History* 68, no. 4: 951–996.

Kirkpatrick, S. A., and Locke, E. A. 1991. "Leadership: Do Traits Matter?" *Academy of Management Executive* 5, no. 2: 48–60.

Kleinedler, S. R., ed. 2016. *Webster's New World Dictionary*, 5th ed. Boston: Houghton Mifflin Harcourt.

Kleinedler, S., ed. 2018. *Webster's New World College Dictionary,* 5th ed. Boston: Houghton Mifflin Harcourt. Original work published 2014.

Kochan, T. A.; Schmidt, S. M.; and DeCotiis, T. A. 1975. "Superior-Subordinate Relations: Leadership and Headship". *Human Relations* 28, no. 3: 279–294.

Kodish, S. 2006. "The Paradoxes of Leadership: The Contribution of Aristotle." *Leadership* 2:451–468.

Koehne, S. 2013. "Nazi Germany as a Christian State: The Protestant Experience of 1933 in Wurttemberg." *Central European History* 46, no. 1: 97–123.

Komives, S. R.; Lucas, N.; and McMahon, T. R. 1998. *Exploring Leadership: For College Students Who Want to Make a Difference.* San Francisco: Jossey-Bass.

Komives, S. R.; Lucas, N.; and McMahon, T. R. 2013. *Exploring Leadership: For College Students Who Want to Make a Difference*, 3rd ed. San Francisco: Jossey-Bass.

Kort, E. D. 2008. "What, After All, Is Leadership? 'Leadership' and Plural Action." *Leadership Quarterly* 9, no. 4: 409–425.

Kotter, J. P. 1988. *The Leadership Factor*. New York: Free.

Kouzes, J. M., and Posner, B. Z. 1990. "The Credibility Factor: What Followers Expect from Their Leaders." *Management Review* 79, no. 1: 29–33.

Kouzes, J. M., and Posner, B. Z. 2003a. "Leadership Is in the Eye of the Follower." In J. Gordon, ed., *Pfeiffer's Classic Activities for Developing Leaders: The Most Enduring, Effective, and Valuable Training Activities for Developing Leaders*, 3–10. New York: John Wiley and Sons.

Kouzes, J. M., and Posner, B. Z. 2003b. *The Leadership Challenge: How to Make Extraordinary Things Happen in Organizations*, 3rd ed. San Francisco: Jossey-Bass.

Kouzes, J. M., and Posner, B. Z. 2016. *Learning Leadership: The Five Fundamentals of Becoming an Exemplary Leader*. San Francisco: Wiley.

Krech, D., and Crutchfield, R. S. 1948. *Theory and Problems of Social Psychology*. New York: McGraw Hill.

Laloggia, J. 2019. "6 Facts about US Political Independents." Pew Research Center. https://www.pewresearch.org/fact-tank/2019/05/15/facts-about-us-political-independents/.

Landau, S. I. 2001. *Dictionaries: The Art and Craft of Lexicography*, 2nd ed. Cambridge, England: University Press.

Landau, S. I. 2009. "Major American Dictionaries." In A. P. Cowie, ed., *The Oxford History of English Lexicography*, 1:182–229. Oxford: Clarendon.

Lapierre, L. M. 2014. "How and Why Should Subordinates Follow Their Managers?" In L. M. Lapierre and M. K. Carsten, eds., *Followership: What Is It and Why Do People Follow?*, 157–169. Bingley: Emerald.

Lapierre, L. M., and Carsten, M. K. 2014. "Introduction and Book Overview." In L. M. Lapierre and M. K. Carsten, eds., *Followership: What Is It and Why Do People Follow?*, ix–xiii. Bingley: Emerald.

Larson, A. 1968. *Eisenhower: The President Nobody Knew*. New York: Charles Scribner's Sons.

Lawler, E. E., and Suttle, J. L. 1972. "A Causal Correlational Test of the Need Hierarchy Concept." *Organizational Behavior and Human Performance* 7, no. 2: 265–287.

Lawless, J. L. 2012. *Becoming a Candidate: Political Ambition and the Decision to Run for Office*. New York: Cambridge University Press.

Lee, S. M., and Farh, C. I. 2019. "Dynamic Leadership Emergence: Differential Impact of Members' and Peers' Contributions in the Idea Generation and Idea Enactment Phases of Innovation Project Teams." *Journal of Applied Psychology* 104, no. 3: 411–432.

Levi, D. 2001. *Group Dynamics for Teams*. Thousand Oaks, CA: SAGE.

Levi, D. 2011. *Group Dynamics for Teams*, 3rd ed. Thousand Oaks, CA: SAGE.

Lim, C. S. H., and Snyder, J. M., Jr. 2012. "Elections and the Quality of Public Officials: Evidence from US State Courts." Working paper 18355. Retrieved from *National Bureau of Economic Research*. http://www.nber.org/papers/w18355.

Lobo, M. C. 2014. "Party and Electoral Leadership." In R. A. W. Rhodes and P. 't Hart, eds., *The Oxford Handbook of Political Leadership*, 362–375. Oxford: Oxford University Press.

Lombardi, V. 1969. "Lombardi's Farewell Speech, Given February 26, 1969, in Janesville, Wisconsin." In P. Hornung and P. Reed, *Lombardi and Me: Players, Coaches, and Colleagues Talk about the Man and the Myth*, 141–153. Chicago: Triumph, 2006.

Long, N. E. 1963. "The Political Act as an Act of Will." *American Journal of Sociology* 69, no. 1: 1–6.

Lord, R. G.; Brown, D. J.; and Harvey, J. L. 2001. "System Constraints on Leadership Perceptions, Behavior, and Influence: An Example of Connectionist Level Processes." In M. A. Hogg and R. S. Tindale, eds., *Blackwell Handbook of Social Psychology: Group Processes*, 283–310. Oxford: Blackwell.

Lord, R. G., and Maher, K. J. 1991. *Leadership and Information Processing: Linking Perceptions and Performance*. Boston: Unwin Hyman.

Lowe, K. B. 2004. "Cross-cultural Leadership." In G. R. Goethals, G. J. Sorenson, and J. M. Burns, eds., *Encyclopedia of Leadership*, 1:300–306. Thousand Oaks, CA: SAGE.

Lussier, R. N., and Achua, C. F. 2007. *Leadership: Theory, Application, and Skill Development*, 3rd ed. Mason, OH: Thomson South-Western.

Lussier, R. N., and Achua, C. F. 2010. *Leadership: Theory, Application, and Skill Development*, 4th ed. Mason, OH: South-Western Cengage Learning.

Mackenzie, K. D. 2010. "Turf Disputes within Federal Systems: Leadership amidst Enforceable Checks and Balances." *Leadership Quarterly* 21, no. 6: 1050–1068.

Magaziner, I. C., and Hout, T. M. 1980. *Japanese Industrial Policy*. Berkeley, CA: Institute of International Studies University of CA.

Magleby, D. B.; Nelson, C. J.; and Westlye, M. C. 2011. "The Myth of the Independent Voter Revisited." In P. M. Sniderman and B. Highton, eds., *Facing the Challenge of Democracy: Explorations in the Analysis of Public Opinion and Political Participation*, 238–263. Princeton, NJ: Princeton University Press.

Manlove, J. 1741. *A New Dictionary of All Such English Words*. Printed for J. Wilcox.

Manning, G., and Curtis, K. 2015. *The Art of Leadership*, 5th ed. New York: McGraw Hill.

Marieta, J. R.; Bagus, T.; and Riantoputra, C. D. 2019. "Conflict Management in Extractive Industries in Indonesia: Leaders-Followers Dynamic to Achieve Perceived Social Justice in Communities." In H. E. Schockman, V. A. Hernandez Soto, and A. Boitano De Moras, eds., *Peace, Reconciliation, and Social Justice Leadership in the 21*st *Century: The Role of Leaders and Followers*, 105–109. Bingley: Emerald.

Marion, R., and Uhl-Bien, M. 2001. "Leadership in Complex Organizations." *Leadership Quarterly* 12, no. 4: 389–418.

Markus, M. J.; Allison, S. T.; and Eylon, D. 2004. Social Psychology: Social Psychology's Definition of Leadership. In G. R. Goethals, G. J. Sorenson, and J. M. Burns, eds., *Encyclopedia of Leadership*, 4:1462–1465. Thousand Oaks, CA: Sage.

Martin, B. 1749. *Lingua Britannica Reformata*. Printed for J. Hodges, S. Austen, J. Newbery, J. Ward, R. Raikes, J. Leake, W. Frederick, and B. Collins.

Marturano, A.; Wren, J. T.; and Harvey, M. 2013. "Editorial: The Making of *Leadership and the Humanities*." *Leadership and the Humanities* 1, no. 1: 1–5. DOI:10.4337/lath.2013.01.00.

Maslow, A. H. 1943. "A Theory of Human Motivation." *Psychological Review* 50, no. 4: 370–396.

Maxwell, J. C. 1998. *The 21 Irrefutable Laws of Leadership: Follow Them and People Will Follow You*. Nashville: Thomas Nelson.

Maxwell, J. C. 2013. *The 5 Levels of Leadership: Proven Steps to Maximize Your Potential*. New York: Center Street.

McCauley, C. D. 2010. "Concepts of Leadership." In E. Biech, ed., *The ASTD Leadership Handbook*, 1–10. Alexandria, VA: ASTD.

McCauley, C., and Fick-Cooper, L. 2015. *Direction, Alignment, Commitment: Achieving Better Results through Leadership*. n.p.: Center for Creative Leadership.

McClelland, D. C. 1970. "The Two Faces of Power.: *Journal of International Relations* 24, no. 1: 29–47.

McClelland, D. C. 1975. *Power: The Inner Experience*. New York: Irvington.

McClelland, D. C. 1985. *Human Motivation*. Glenview, IL: Scott, Foresman.

McCrimmon, M. 2011. "The Ideal Leader." *Ivey Business Journal*. Retrieved February 22, 2020. https://iveybusinessjournal. com/publication/the-ideal-leader/.

McFarland, L. J.; Senn, L. E.; and Childress, J. R. 1993. *21ˢᵗ Century Leadership: Dialogues with 100 Top Leaders*. Los Angeles: Leadership.

Medina, M. 2011. "Leadership and the Process of Becoming: An Artist Never Paints the Same Picture Twice." *Existential Analysis* 22, no. 1: 70–82.

Meindl, J. R. 1990. "On Leadership: An Alternative to the Conventional Wisdom." In G. R. Goethals, G. J. Sorenson, and J. M. Burns, eds., *Research in Organizational Behavior: An Annual Series of Analytical Essays and Critical Reviews*, 12:159–203. Greenwich, CT: JAI.

Meindl, J. R. 1993. "Reinventing Leadership: A Radical, Social Psychological Approach." In J. K. Murnighan, ed., *Social Psychology in Organizations*, 89–118. Englewood Cliffs, NJ: Prentice Hall.

Meindl, J. R. 1995. "The Romance of Leadership as a Follower-Centric Theory: A Social Constructionist Approach." *Leadership Quarterly* 6, no. 3: 329–341.

Meindl, J. R.; Ehrlich, S. B.; and Dukerich, J. M. 1985. "The Romance of Leadership." *Administrative Science Quarterly* 30, no. 1: 78–102.

Meindl, J. R.; Pastor, J. C.; and Mayo, M. 2004. "Romance of Leadership." In G. R. Goethals, G. J. Sorenson, and J. M. Burns, eds., *Encyclopedia of Leadership*, 3:1347–1351. Thousand Oaks, CA: SAGE.

Merriam-Webster. n.d. "How Long Has Merriam-Webster Been Publishing Dictionaries?" *Merriam-Webster.com*. Retrieved April 17, 2021. https://www.merriam-webster.com/about us/faq.

Merriam-Webster. n.d. "Leadership." *Merriam-Webster.com*. Retrieved May 1, 2021. https://www.merriam-webster.com/dictionary/leadership.

Michaelis, R. R., ed. 1963. *Funk and Wagnalls Standard College Dictionary*, text ed. New York: Harcourt, Brace, and World.

Micklethwait, D. 2000. *Noah Webster and the American Dictionary*. Jefferson, NC: McFarland.

Middlebrooks, A.; Allen, S. J.; McNutt, M. S.; and Morrison, J. L. 2020. *Discovering Leadership: Designing Your Success*. Thousand Oaks, CA: SAGE.

Miller, D., and Sardais, C. 2011. "A Concept of Leadership for Strategic Organization." *Strategic Organization* 9, no. 2: 174–184.

Mish, F. C., ed. 1983. *Webster's Ninth New Collegiate Dictionary*. Springfield, MA: Merriam-Webster.

Mish, F. C., ed. 1994. *Merriam-Webster's Collegiate Dictionary*, 10th ed. Springfield, MA: Merriam-Webster. Original work published 1993.

Mish, F. C., ed. 2014. *Merriam-Webster's Collegiate Dictionary*, 11th ed. Springfield, MA: Merriam-Webster. Original work published 2003.

Mitroff, I. 1978. "Systemic Problem Solving." In M. W. McCall Jr. and M. M. Lombardo, eds., *Leadership: Where Else Can We Go?*, 129–143. Durham, NC: Duke University Press.

Moltchanova, A. 2015. "Rulers, Moralities and Leadership." In J. Boaks and M. Levine, eds., *Leadership and Ethics*, 47–72. London: Bloomsbury.

Montgomery, B. L. 1961. *The Path to Leadership*. St James Place, London: Collins.

Moore, B. V. 1927. "The May Conference on Leadership." *Personnel Journal* 5 (June): 124–128.

Morris, V. M. 2019. "The Impact Leadership Styles Have on Organizational Performance: A Correlation Study on Local Public Administrators." Doctoral dissertation, Northcentral University. ProQuest Dissertations.

Morris, W., ed. 1969. *The American Heritage Dictionary of the English Language*. Boston: Houghton Mifflin.

Mumford, E. 1906. "The Origins of Leadership." *American Journal of Sociology* 12, no. 2: 216–240.

Mumford, M. D. 2011. "A Hale Farewell: The State of Leadership Research." *Leadership Quarterly* 22, no. 1: 1–7.

Mumford, M. D.; Zaccaro, S. J.; Connelly, M. S.; and Marks, M. A. 2000. "Leadership Skills: Conclusions and Future Directions." *Leadership Quarterly* 11, no. 1: 155–170.

Mumford, M. D.; Zaccaro, S. J.; Harding, F. D.; Jacobs, T. O.; and Fleishman, E. A. 2000. "Leadership Skills for a Changing World: Solving Complex Social Problems." *Leadership Quarterly* 11, no. 1:11–35.

Munson, E. L. 1921. *The Management of Men: A Handbook on the Systematic Development of Morale and the Control of Human Behavior*. New York: Henry Holt.

Murphy, S. E., and Johnson, S. K. 2011. "The Benefits of a Long-Term Approach to Leadership Development: Understanding the Seeds of Leadership." *Leadership Quarterly* 22, no. 3: 459–470.

Murphy, S. E.; Reichard, R. J.; and Johnson, S. K. 2008. "Self-Regulation and Leadership: Implications for Leader Performance and Leader Development." In J. B. Ciulla, C. Hoyt, G. R. Goethals, and D. R. Forsyth, eds., *Leadership at the Crossroads*, 1:250–264. Westport, CTN: Praeger.

Murray, J. A. H.; Bradley, H.; and Craigie, W. A., eds. 1908. A *New English Dictionary on Historical Principles,* Vol. 6. Oxford: Clarendon.

Murrell, K. L. 1997. "Emergent Theories of Leadership for the Next Century" *Toward Relational Concepts* 15, no. 3: 35–42.

Nahavandi, A. 2009. *The Art and Science of Leadership*, 5th ed. Upper Saddle River, NJ: Pearson Education.

Nanus, B. 1989. *The Leader's Edge: The Seven Keys to Leadership in a Turbulent World.* Chicago: Contemporary.

Nazeemudeen, Z. M. 2019. "Women Can Make a Difference in Economic Marginalization and Women's Right to Equality in Post-conflict Context of Sri Lanka: Revival of Challenges and a Perspective Beyond the UNRSC 1325." In H. E. Schockman, V. A. Hernandez Soto, and A. Boitano De Moras., eds., *Peace, Reconciliation, and Social Justice Leadership in the 21st Century: The Role of Leaders and Followers*, 42–48. Bingley: Emerald.

Newcomb, T. M.; Turner, R. H.; and Converse, P. E. 1965. *Social Psychology: The Study of Human Interaction.* New York: Holt, Rinehart, and Winston.

Nitze, P. H. 1954. "The United States in the Face of the Communist Challenge." In C. G. Haines, ed., *The Threat of Soviet Imperialism*, 372–379. Baltimore: Johns Hopkins University Press.

Northouse, P. G. 1997. *Leadership: Theory and Practice*. Thousand Oaks, CA: SAGE.

Northouse, P. G. 2022. *Leadership: Theory and Practice*, 9th ed. Thousand Oaks, CA: SAGE.

Northup, N. 1987. "Local Nonpartisan Elections, Political Parties and the First Amendment." *Columbia Law Review* 87, no. 8: 1677–1701.

Nye, J. S., Jr. 2008. *The Powers to Lead*. New York: Oxford University Press.

O'Connell, P. K. 2014. "A Simplified Framework for 21st Century Leader Development." *Leadership Quarterly* 25, no. 2: 183–203.

Osborn, R. N., and Hunt, J. G. 1975. "An Adaptive-Reactive Theory of Leadership: The Role of Macro Variables in Leadership Research." In J. G. Hunt and L. L. Larson, es., *Leadership Frontiers*, 27–44. Kent, OH: Kent State University Comparative Administration Research Institute.

Osborn, R. N.; Hunt, J. G.; and Jauch, L. R. 2002. "Toward a Contextual Theory of Leadership." *Leadership Quarterly* 13, no. 6: 797–837.

Ospina, S. M., and Hittleman, M. 2011. "Thinking Sociologically about Leadership." In M. Harvey and R. E. Riggio, eds., *Leadership Studies: The Dialogue of Disciplines*, 89–100. Cheltenham: Edward Elgar.

Ospina, S.; Godsoe, B.; Schall, E.; and Dodge, J. 2002. "Co-producing Knowledge: Practitioners and Scholars Working Together to Understand Leadership." In C. Cherrey and L. R. Matusak, es., *Building Leadership Bridges 2002*, 59–67. College Park, MD: James MacGregor Burns Academy of Leadership.

Oxford University Press. 2000-. "Leadership, n." *Oxford English Dictionary Online*. Retrieved January 31, 2002. https://www-oed-com.ezproxy.neu.edu/view/Entry/106604?redirectedFrom=leadership#eid). Acc

Padilla, A. 2012. *Leadership: Leaders, Followers, Environments*. New York: John Wiley and Sons.

Paige, G. D. 1977. *The Scientific Study of Political Leadership*. New York: Free.

Parsons, D. A. 2007. "Christian Hope as a Factor in How Protestant Christians Followed Hitler." Unpublished doctoral dissertation, Drew University.

Perruci, G. 2011. "Millennials and Globalization: The Cross-cultural Challenge of Intragenerational Leadership." *Journal of Leadership Studies* 5, no. 3: 82–87.

Peters, T., and Austin, N. 1985. *A Passion for Excellence: The Leadership Difference*. New York: Random House.

Peters, T. J., and Waterman, R. H. 1982. *In Search of Excellence: Lessons from America's Best-Run Companies*. New York: Harper and Row.

Pfeffer, J. 1977. "The Ambiguity of Leadership." *Academy of Management Review* 2, no. 1: 104–112.

Pfeffer, J. 1978. "The Ambiguity of Leadership." In M. W. McCall Jr. and M. M. Lombardo, eds., *Leadership: Where Else Can We Go?*, 13–34. Durham, NC: Duke University Press.

Phillips, E. 1658. *The New World of English Words: Or, a General Dictionary*. E. Tyler for Nath. Brooke.

Phillips, T. R. 1939. "Leader and Led." *Coast Artillery Journal* 82, no. 1: 48–57.

Pickett, J. P., ed. 2000. *The American Heritage Dictionary of the English Language*, 4th ed. Boston: Houghton Mifflin.

Pickett, J. P., ed. 2018. *The American Heritage Dictionary of the English Language*, 5th ed. Boston: Houghton Mifflin Harcourt. Original work published 2011.

Pietraszewski, D. 2020. "The Evolution of Leadership: Leadership and Followership as a Solution to the Problem of Creating and Executing Successful Coordination and Cooperation Enterprises." *Leadership Quarterly* 31, no. 2: 1–12. https://www-sciencedirect-com.ezproxy.neu.edu/science/article/pii/S1048984318302765.

Pigors, P. 1934. "Types of Followers." *Journal of Social Psychology* 5, no. 3: 378–383.

Pigors, P. 1935. *Leadership or Domination*. New York: Houghton Mifflin.

Pondy, L. R. 1978. "Leadership Is a Language Game." In M. W. McCall Jr. and M. M. Lombardo, eds., *Leadership: Where Else Can We Go?*, 87–99. Durham, NC: Duke University Press.

Porter, N., ed. 1890. *Webster's International Dictionary*. Springfield, MA: G. and C. Merriam.

Porter, M. E. 1980. *Competitive Strategy: Techniques for Analyzing Industries and Competitors*. New York: Free.

Porter, M. E. 1985. *Competitive Advantage: Creating and Sustaining Superior Performance*. New York: Free.

Porter, M. E. 1990. *The Competitive Advantage of Nations*. New York: Free.

Prcic, T. 2008. "Suffixes vs. Final Combining Forms in English: A Lexicographic Perspective." *International Journal of Lexicography* 21, no. 1: 1–22.

Prentice, W. C. H. 1961. "Understanding Leadership." *Harvard Business Review* 39, no. 5: 143–151.

Punj, A., and Krishnan, V. R. 2006. "Transformational Leadership and Altruism: Role of Power Distance in a High Power Distance Culture." In *Proceedings of the Annual Conference of the Administrative Sciences Association of Canada*, 1–14. https://citeseerx.ist.psu.edu/viewdoc/download?doi=10.1.1.524.8763&rep=rep1&type=pdf. Accessed January 27, 2022.

Pye, A. 2005. "Leadership and Organizing: Sensemaking in Action." *Leadership* 1, no. 1: 31–49.

Raelin, J. 2006. "Does Action Learning Promote Collaborative Leadership?" *Academy of Management Learning and Education* 5, no. 2: 152–168.

Rakich, N., and Best, R. 2020. "There Wasn't That Much Split-Ticket Voting in 2020." FiveThirtyEight Politics, December 2. https://fivethirtyeight.com/features/there-wasnt-that-much-split-ticket-voting-in-2020/.

Rauch, C. F., Jr., and Behling, O. 1984. "Functionalism: Basis for an Alternate Approach to the Study of Leadership." In J. G. Hunt, D. M. Hosking, C. A. Schriesheim, and R. Stewart, eds., *Leaders and Managers: International Perspectives on Managerial Behavior and Leadership*, 45–62. Elmsford, NY: Pergamon.

Reagan, R. 1983a. *Statement on Establishment of the President's Commission on Industrial Competitiveness.* Ronald Reagan Presidential Library and Museum. https://www.reaganlibrary.gov/archives/speech/statement-establishment-presidents-commission-industrial-competitiveness. Accessed January 27, 2022.

Reagan, R. 1983b. *Appointment of 20 Members of the President's Commission on Industrial Competitiveness.* The American Presidency Project. https://www.presidency.ucsb.edu/documents/appointment-20-members-the-presidents-commission-industrial-competitiveness. Accessed January 27, 2022.

Rego, L.; Mohono, K.; and Peter, G. M. 2019. "Beyond Ubunto: What the World Can Learn about Building Community from Africa." In H. E. Schockman, V. A. Hernandez Soto, and A. Boitano De Moras, eds., *Peace, Reconciliation, and Social Justice Leadership in the 21ˢᵗ Century: The Role of Leaders and Followers*, 95–102. Bingley: Emerald.

Reiche, B. S.; Bird, A.; Mendenhall, M. E.; and Osland, J. S. 2017. "Contextualizing Leadership: A Typology of Global Leadership Roles." *Journal of International Business Studies* 48, no. 5: 552–572.

Reuter, E. B. 1941. *Handbook of Sociology*. New York: Dryden.

Rhodes, R. A. W., and 't Hart, P. 2014. "Puzzles of Political Leadership." In R. A. W. Rhodes and P. 't Hart, eds., *The Oxford Handbook of Political Leadership*, 2–21. Oxford: Oxford University Press.

Ridgeway, C. L. 2003. "Status Characteristics and Leadership." In D. van Knippenberg and M. A. Hogg, eds. *Leadership and Power: Identity Processes in Groups and Organizations*, 65–78. Thousand Oaks, CA: SAGE.

Riggio, R. E. 2008. *Introduction to Industrial/Organizational Psychology*, 5ᵗʰ ed. Upper Saddle River, NJ: Prentice Hall.

Riggio, R. E. 2011. "The Management Perspective: Engineering Effective Leadership in Organizations." In M. Harvey and R. E. Riggio, eds., *Leadership Studies: The Dialogue of Disciplines*, 119–128. Cheltenham: Edward Elgar.

Robbins, S. P., and Coulter, M. 2003. *Management*, 7ᵗʰ updated ed.. Upper Saddle River, NJ: Prentice Hall.

Robbins, S. P., and Coulter, M. 2018. *Management*, 14th ed. New York: Pearson.

Rodgers, R. K., and Bligh, M. C. 2014. "Exploring the 'Flip Side' of the Coin: Do Authentic Leaders Need Authentic Followers?" In L. M. Lapierre and M. K. Carsten, eds., *Followership: What Is It and Why Do People Follow?*, 27–45. Bingley: Emerald.

Rokeach, M. 1968. *Beliefs, Attitudes, and Values: A Theory of Organization and Change*. San Francisco: Jossey-Bass.

Rokeach, M. 1971. "Long-Range Experimental Modification of Values, Attitudes and Behavior." *American Psychologist* 26, no. 5: 453–459.

Rokeach, M. 1973. *The Nature of Human Values*. New York: Free.

Rooney, K., and Soukhanov, A. 2004. *Encarta Webster's Dictionary of the English Language*, 2nd ed. New York: Bloomsbury.

Rost, J. C. 1991. *Leadership for the Twenty-First Century*. New York: Praeger.

Rost, J. C. 1993. "Leadership Development in the New Millennium." *Journal of Leadership Studies* 1, no. 1: 91–110.

Rost, J. 2008. "Followership: An Outmoded Concept." In R. E. Riggio, I. Chaleff, and J. Lipman-Blumen, eds., *The Art of Followership: How Great Followers Create Great Leaders and Organizations*, 53–64. San Francisco: Jossey-Bass.

Rost, J. C., and Barker, R. A. 2000. "Leadership Education in Colleges: Toward a 21st Century Paradigm." *Journal of Leadership Studies* 7, no. 1: 3–12.

Rousseau, D. 1995. *Psychological Contracts in Organizations: Understanding Written and Unwritten Agreements*. Thousand Oaks, CA: SAGE.

Ruben, B. D., and Gigliotti, R. A. 2017. "Communication: Sine Qua Non of Organizational Leadership Theory and Practice." *International Journal of Business Communication* 54, no. 1: 12–30.

Rushton, J. P.; Chrisjohn, R. D.; and Fekken, G. C. 1981. "The Altruistic Personality and the Self Report Altruism Scale." *Personality and Individual Differences* 2, no. 4: 293–302.

Saghal, P., and Pathak, A. 2007. "Transformational Leaders: Their Socialization, Self-Concept, and Shaping Experiences." *International Journal of Leadership Studies* 2, no. 3: 263–279.

Salovaara, P., and Ropo, A. 2013. "Embodied Learning Experience in Leadership Development." In L. R. Melina, G. J. Burgess, L. L. Falkman, and A. Marturano, eds., *The Embodiment of Leadership*, 193–215. San Francisco: Jossey-Bass.

Sarkesian, S. C. 1981. "A Personal Perspective." In J. H. Buck and L. J. Korb, eds., *Military Leadership*, 243–247. Beverly Hills, CA: SAGE

Satyanath, S.; Voigtlaender, N.; and Voth, H.-J. 2013. "Bowling for Fascism: Social Capital and the Rise of the Nazi Party." *Journal of Political Economy* 125, no. 2: 478–526.

Saunders, W. 2003. "Cross and Swastika: The Nazi Party and the German Churches." *History Review* 46:9–14.

Schaffner, B. F.; Streb, M.; and Wright, G. 2001. "Teams without Uniforms: The Nonpartisan Ballot in State and Local Elections." *Political Research Quarterly* 54, no. 1: 7–30.

Schein, E. H. 1985. *Organizational Culture and Leadership: A Dynamic View*. San Francisco: Jossey-Bass.

Schenk, C. 1928. "Leadership: An Introductory Outline." *Infantry Journal* 33, no. 2: 111–122.

Schuyler, K. G. 2016. "Visions of a Healthy World: Views from Thought Leaders." In K. G. Schuyler, J. E. Baugher, and K. Jironet, eds., *Creative Social Change: Leadership for a Healthy World*, 23–90. Bingley: Emerald.

Scott, J. N., and Bailey, N. 1755. *A New Universal Etymological English Dictionary*. Printed for T. Osborne and J. Shipton, J. Hodges, R. Baldwin, W. Johnston, and J. Ward.

Seeman, M. 1960. *Social Status and Leadership: The Case of the School Executive*. Columbus: Ohio State University Bureau of Educational Research.

Shamir, B. 2004. "Followers, Motivation of." In G. R. Goethals, G. J. Sorenson, and J. M. Burns, eds., *Encyclopedia of Leadership*, 2:499–504. Thousand Oaks, CA: SAGE.

Shamir, B. 2007. "From Passive Recipients to Active Co-producers: Followers' Roles in the Leadership Process." In B. Shamir, R. Pillai, M. C. Bligh, and M. Uhl-Bien, eds., *Follower-Centered Perspectives on Leadership: A Tribute to the Memory of James R. Meindl*, ix–xxxix. Greenwich, CN: Information Age.

Shamir, B., and Howell, J. M. 1999. "Organizational and Contextual Influences on the Emergence and Effectiveness of Charismatic Leadership." *Leadership Quarterly* 10, no. 2: 257–283.

Shaw, M. E. 1981. *Group Dynamics: The Psychology of Small Group Behavior,* 3rd ed. New York: McGraw Hill.

Sher, M. 2004. "Psychoanalytic Theory." In G. R. Goethals, G. J. Sorenson, and J. M. Burns, eds., *Encyclopedia of Leadership,* 3:1259–1265. Thousand Oaks, CA: SAGE.

Shore, C. 2014. "Anthropology." In R. A. W. Rhodes and P. 't Hart, eds., *The Oxford Handbook of Political Leadership,* 176–192. Oxford: Oxford University Press.

Silva, A. 2016. "What Is Leadership?" *Journal of Business Studies Quarterly* 8, no. 1: 1–5.

Sims, H. P., Jr., and Manz, C. C. 1984. "Observing Leader Verbal Behavior: Toward Reciprocal Determinism in Leadership Theory." *Journal of Applied Psychology* 69, no. 2: 222–232.

Simpson, J. A., and Weiner, E. S. C., eds. 1991. *The Oxford English Dictionary,* 2nd ed., Vol. 8. Oxford: Clarendon. Original work published 1989.

Slatter, S. 1984. *Corporate Recovery: A Guide to Turnaround Management.* Harmondsworth: Penguin.

Smircich, L., and Morgan, G. 1982. "Leadership: The Management of Meaning." *Journal of Applied Behavior Science* 18, no. 3: 257–273.

Soper, B.; Milford, G. E.; and Rosenthal, G. T. 1995. "Belief When Evidence Does Not Support Theory." *Psychology and Marketing* 12, no. 5: 415–422.

Sorial, S. 2015. "Authority and Leadership: The Ethical Obligations of Authority." In J. Boaks and M. Levine, eds., *Leadership and Ethics*, 73–94. London: Bloomsbury.

Soukhanov, A. H., ed. 1992. *The American Heritage Dictionary of the English Language*. 3rd ed. Boston: Houghton Mifflin.

Spenkuch, J. L., and Tillman, P. 2018. "Elite Influence? Religion and the Electoral Success of the Nazis." *American Journal of Political Science* 62, no. 1: 19–36.

Springborg, C. 2010. "Leadership as Art—Leaders Coming to Their Senses." *Leadership* 6, no. 3: 243–258.

Stainton Rogers, W. 2011. *Social Psychology*, 2nd ed. Maidenhead: McGraw Hill Open University Press.

Starnes, D. T., and Noyes, G. E. 1946. *The English Dictionary from Cawdrey to Johnson 1604–1755*. Chapel Hill, NC: University of North Carolina Press.

Stech, E. L. 2008. "A New Leadership-Followership Paradigm." In R. E. Riggio, I. Chaleff, and J. Lipman-Blumen, eds., *The Art of Followership: How Great Followers Create Great Leaders and Organizations*, 41–52. San Francisco: Jossey-Bass.

Stein, J., and Urdang, L., eds. 1966. *The Random House Dictionary of the English Language*. New York: Random House.

Steger, S. A. 1913. *American Dictionaries: A Dissertation*. Baltimore: J. H. Furst.

Stogdill, R. M. 1950. "Leadership, Membership, and Organizations." *Psychological Bulletin* 47, no. 1: 1–14.

Stogdill, R. M. 1974. *Handbook of Leadership: A Survey of Theory and Research*. New York: Free.

Stovall, J. G. 2005. *Journalism: Who, What, When, Where, Why and How*. Boston: Allyn and Bacon.

Sturm, R. E., and Monzani, L. 2018. "Power and Leadership." In J. Antonakis and D. V. Day, eds., *The Nature of Leadership*, 3rd ed., 272–299. Thousand Oaks, CA: SAGE.

Sullivan, L. E. 2009. *The SAGE Glossary of the Social and Behavioral Sciences*. Thousand Oaks, CA: SAGE.

Tannenbaum, R.; Weschler, I. R.; and Massarik, F. 1961. *Leadership and Organization: A Behavioral Science Approach*. New York: McGraw Hill.

Tead, O. 1929. *Human Nature and Management: The Applications of Psychology to Executive Leadership*. New York: McGraw Hill.

Tead, O. 1935. *The Art of Leadership*. New York: McGraw Hill.

Tenpas, K. D. 2021. "Tracking Turnover in the Trump Administration." Brookings Institution. https://www.brookings.edu/research/tracking-turnover-in-the-trump-administration/.

Thibaut, J. W., and Kelley, H. H. 1959. *The Social Psychology of Groups*. New York: John Wiley and Sons.

Thoroughgood, C. N.; Sawyer, K. B.; Padilla, A.; and Lunsford, L. 2016. "Destructive Leadership: A Critique of Leader-Centric Perspectives and toward a More Holistic Definition." *Journal of Business Ethics* 151, no. 3: 627–649.

Training Industry. 2019. "Leadership: The Leadership Training Market." Accessed June 12, 2021. https://trainingindustry.com/wiki/leadership/the-leadership-training-market/.

Tse, H. H. M.; Huang, X.; and Lam, W. 2013. "Why Does Transformational Leadership Matter for Employee Turnover? A Multi-foci Social Exchange Perspective." *Leadership Quarterly* 24, no. 5: 763–776.

Ulmer, W. F., Jr. 2017. *A Military Leadership Notebook: Principles into Practice*. Bloomington, IN: iUniverse.

Underdal, A. 1994. "Leadership Theory: Rediscovering the Arts of Management." In I. W. Zartman, ed., *International Multilateral Negotiations: Approaches to the Management of Complexity*, 178–197. San Francisco: Jossey-Bass.

University of San Diego. n.d. "Colleges and Schools: School of Leadership and Education Sciences." Accessed May 13, 2021. https://www.sandiego.edu/academics/college-and-schools.php.

Urdang, L. 1968. *The Random House Dictionary of the English Language, College Edition*. New York: Random House.

Urwich, L. F. 1961. "Management and Human Relations." In R. Tannenbaum, I. R. Weschler, and F. Massarik. *Leadership and Organization: A Behavioral Science Approach,* 416–428. New York: McGraw Hill.

Van Vugt, M. 2006. "Evolutionary Origins of Leadership and Followership." *Personality and Social Psychology Review* 10, no. 4: 354–371.

Van Vugt, M. 2012. "The Nature in Leadership: Evolutionary, Biological, and Social Neuroscience Perspectives." In D. V. Day and J. Antonakis, eds., *The Nature of Leadership*, 2nd ed., 141–175. Thousand Oaks, CA: SAGE.

Van Vugt, M. 2018. "Evolutionary, Biological, and Neuroscience Perspectives." In J. Antonakis and D. V. Day, eds. *The Nature of Leadership*, 3rd ed., 189–217. Thousand Oaks, CA: SAGE.

Van Vugt, M.; Hogan, R.; and Kaiser, R. B. 2008. "Leadership, Followership, and Evolution: Some Lessons from the Past." *American Psychologist* 63, no. 3: 182–196.

Varney, J. 2009. "Leadership as Meaning-Making." *Human Resource Management International Digest* 17, no. 5: 3–5.

Vizetelly, F. H., ed. 1922. *The College Standard Dictionary of the English Language*. New York: Funk and Wagnalls.

Voigtlaender, N., and Voth, H.-J. 2019. *Highway to Hitler*. Working Paper 20150. https://www.nber.org/papers/w20150.

Von Rueden, C., and Van Vugt, M. 2015. "Leadership in Small-Scale Societies: Some Implications for Theory, Research, and Practice." *Leadership Quarterly* 26, no. 6: 978–990.

Vroom, V. H. 1964. *Work and Motivation*. New York: John Wiley and Sons.

Vroom, V. H., and Jago, A. G. 2007. "The Role of the Situation in Leadership." *American Psychologist* 62, no. 1: 17–24.

Wahba, M. A., and Bridwell, L. G. 1976. "Maslow Reconsidered: A Review of Research on the Need Hierarchy Theory." *Organizational Behavior and Human Performance* 15, no. 2: 265–287.

Waldman, D. A.; Carter, M. Z.; and Hom, P. W. 2015. "A Multilevel Investigation of Leadership and Turnover Behavior." *Journal of Management* 41, no. 6: 1724–1744.

Waldman, D. A., and O'Reilly, C. A. 2020. *Leadership for Organizations*. Thousand Oaks, CA: SAGE.

Walker, R., and Aritz, J. 2014. *Leadership Talk: A Discourse Approach to Leader Emergence*. New York: Business Expert.

Walsh, B.; Jamison, S.; and Walsh, C. 2009. *The Score Takes Care of Itself: My Philosophy of Leadership*. New York: Portfolio.

Walters, D. B. 2009. *Exploring a Definition of Leadership and the Biography of Dr. Frank B. Wynn*. Doctoral dissertation, University of Montana. Scholar Works University of Montana.

Watkins, P. 1989. "Leadership, Power and Symbols in Educational Administration." In J. Smyth, ed., *Critical Perspectives on Educational Leadership*, 9–37. London: Palmer.

Webster, N. 1828. *An American Dictionary of the English Language*, Vol. 2. New York: S. Converse.

Webster, N. 1970. *An American Dictionary of the English Language*, Vol. 2. New York: S. Converse. Original work published 1828.

Webster, N. 1841. *An American Dictionary of the English Language: First Edition in Octavo*, Vol. 2–3. New Haven: N. Webster.

Webster, N., and Goodrich, C.A., eds. 1847/1848. *An American Dictionary of the English Language*, 3rd ed. Springfield, MA: George and Charles Merriam.

Webster's Collegiate Dictionary: A Dictionary of the English Language. 1898. Springfield, MA: G. and C. Merriam Co.

Webster's Collegiate Dictionary, 3rd ed. 1916. Springfield, MA: G. and C. Merriam.

Weiss, J. W. 2011. *An Introduction to Leadership*. San Diego: Bridgeport Education.

Whitney, W. D. 1889–1891. *The Century Dictionary: An Encyclopedic Lexicon of the English Language*, Vol. 3. New York: Century.

Wilson, S. 2016. *Thinking Differently about Leadership: A Critical History of Leadership Studies*. Northampton, MA: Edward Elgar.

Wilson, C. L.; O'Hare, D.; and Shipper, F. 1990. "Task Cycle Theory: The Processes of Influence." In K. E. Clark and M. B. Clark. eds., *Measures of Leadership*, 185–204. West Orange, NJ: Leadership Library of America.

Wooden, J. R., and Jamison, S. 2007. *The Essential Wooden: A Lifetime of Lessons on Leaders and Leadership*. New York: McGraw Hill.

Woolf, H. B., ed. 1973. *Webster's New Collegiate Dictionary*, 8th ed. Springfield, MA: Merriam-Webster.

Worcester, J. E. 1846. *A Universal and Critical Dictionary of the English Language.* Boston: Wilkins, Carter.

Worcester, J. E. 1860. *A Dictionary of the English Language.* Boston: Hickling, Swan, and Brewer.

Wren, J. T. 2007. "A Quest for a Grand Theory of Leadership." In G. R. Goethals and G. L. J. Sorenson, eds., *The Quest for a General Theory of Leadership*, 1–38. Cheltenham: Edward Elgar.

Wren, J. T. 2011. "Of History and Leadership: The Discipline of History and the Understanding of Leadership.: In M. Harvey and R. E. Riggio, eds., *Leadership Studies: The Dialogue of Disciplines*, 66–81. Cheltenham: Edward Elgar.

Wren, J. T., and Price, T. L. 2007. "Conclusion." In J. T. Wren and T. L. Price, eds., *The Values of Presidential Leadership*,. 215–226. New York: Palgrave Macmillan.

Yammarino, F. 2013. "Leadership: Past, Present, and Future." *Journal of Leadership and Organizational Studies* 20, no. 2: 149–155.

Young, O. 1991. "Political Leadership and Regime Formation: On the Development of Institutions in International Society." *International Organization* 45, no. 3: 281–309.

Yukl, G. A. 1989a. *Leadership in Organizations*, 2nd ed. Englewood Cliffs, NJ: Prentice Hall.

Yukl, G. A. 1989b. "Managerial Leadership: A Review of Theory and Research." *Journal of Management* 15, no. 2: 251–289.

Yukl, G. A. 1994. *Leadership in Organizations*, 3rd ed. Englewood Cliffs, NJ: Prentice Hall. 400

Yukl, G. A. 1998. *Leadership in Organizations*, 4th ed. Englewood Cliffs, NJ: Prentice Hall.

Yukl, G. A. 2002. *Leadership in Organizations*, 5th ed. Upper Saddle River, NJ: Prentice Hall.

Yukl, G. A. 2006. *Leadership in Organizations*, 6th ed. Upper Saddle River, NJ: Pearson Prentice Hall.

Yukl, G., and Gardner, W. L. 2020. *Leadership in Organizations*, 9th ed. Upper Saddle River, NJ: Pearson.

Yukl, G., and Van Fleet, D. D. 1992. "Theory and Research on Leadership in Organizations." In M. D. Dunnette and L. M. Hough, eds., *Handbook of Industrial and Organizational Psychology*, 2nd ed., 3:147–197. Palo Alto, CA: Consulting Psychologists.

Zastrow, C., and Kirst-Ashman, K. K. 2001. *Understanding Human Behavior and the Social Environment*, 5th ed. Belmont, CA: Brooks/Cole Thomson Learning.

Zhou, L.; Wang, M.; and Vancouver, J. B. 2019. "A Formal Model of Leadership Goal Striving: Development of Core Process Mechanisms and Extensions to Action Team Context." *Journal of Applied Psychology* 104, no. 3: 388–410.

INDEX

ABOUT THE AUTHOR

JOSEPH L. CURTIN has been a management and leadership development consultant since 1984 and has served over one hundred clients in twenty-two states and three Canadian provinces in numerous industries. He has delivered leadership training to over 250 business owners, executives, managers, and supervisors. In addition to leadership development, he has provided management consulting and project management services in various areas. He earned a Ph.D. in management from California Coast University, has master's and bachelor's degrees from Eastern Illinois University, and is the author of seven publications.

Printed in the United States
by Baker & Taylor Publisher Services